IN THE CROSSFIRE
of WAR AND PEACE

An Iranian American Story

FRED ZANDPOUR

ISBN
Paperback 979-8-9910231-0-8
Hard Copy 979-8-9910231-1-5
E-Book 979-8-9910231-2-2

Book Cover by WJ Byrun

I dedicate this book to my wonderful grandchildren.
Sophia, Elliott, Brandon, and Benjamin.

TABLE OF CONTENTS

It was just getting dark as I approached the mosque and I saw a large crowd walking toward me. I immediately knew taking the shortcut was a mistake that day! I had to stop and soon the crowd of mostly young men surrounded my car. I was sure they had just listened to a fiery sermon about the shah's extravagances, corruption, and the oppression of the people; many angry faces who were probably looking for a target peered at me. Clean-shaven and wearing a Cecil Gee suit sitting in my luxury American car and living in the upscale Farmanieh area not too far from the shah's palace, I hardly could fit the bill of a revolutionary.

I got the feeling they planned to break my windows and attack me or possibly burn my car. As they got closer, I thought of Sherry and Mike ready for me to have dinner with them and I was petrified. I decided that sitting and waiting was not an option. I opened the driver's side door and stood on the running board of the large Buick Skylark so I was higher than all of them. In a strong voice, I told them the shah had just left and everyone was celebrating on the streets; the people were looking forward to welcoming Ayatollah Khomeini. As I spoke, I pointed to the poster of Khomeini that the teenager had left on my windshield…

INTRODUCTION

Stories, Symbols, and Straight Talk

Fred was born in Tehran and grew up during a tumultuous period when Iran was struggling to update its identity and culture through modernization and westernization under the shah—with the full support of the United States—while facing fierce resistance from a fanatic and powerful religious establishment. Additionally, there was a constant threat and interference from its northern communist neighbor, the Russians, who had a long record of invading Iran. Like most Iranians, Fred was gradually exposed to American entertainment and its lifestyle; during high school, he was attracted to the freedom, beauty, and glamour of America when he saw the movie *A Summer Place*. His dad, Fazlullah, was a civil servant, and his mother was a modern, poetic housewife; they were both fans of America, and even with their limited resources, helped Fred reach his dream of going to college there.

In 1960s America, Fred once again witnessed the struggle between traditional and modern forces. He was most curious about race relations, the Civil Rights movement, and Vietnam War protests. After five years of observing US counterculture, drifting away from his old values, and becoming somewhat confused and alienated, he returned to Iran while under financial pressure without completing his education. His American dream was shattered; he disappointed his family.

In the 1970s, he enjoyed a peaceful and prosperous Iran where the forces of modernity were dominant and Western movies, music, and fashion were taking hold. In major cities, he saw women in the Islamic hijab going shopping with their daughters in short skirts. Energized by the love and support of his family, Fred discovered talents and capabilities that he never knew he had, managed to earn a bachelor's degree while working in the nascent advertising industry, and was soon running an agency with clients like Exxon, Colgate Palmolive, and Bristol Myers, thanks to Iran's oil revenues and the language and social skills that he had picked up in America.

His agency, Admen-BBDO Advertising, partnered with BBDO (Batten, Barton, Durstine, and Osborn), one of the largest advertising conglomerates in the world. With his beautiful wife, Sherry, by his side and with the arrival of his handsome son, Mike, Fred felt absolutely blessed. However, life as he knew it ended abruptly with the 1979 Islamic Revolution. A smoldering fire suddenly burst into flames channeled by the Shia clerics into the 1979 Islamic Revolution and toppled 2,500 years of monarchical rule. Once again, Iran's identity and culture changed significantly. The revolution disrupted Fred's life, his business, and the regional balance of power and peace in the region; its implications and reverberations are still felt around the world more than four decades later. Iran's peace and prosperity have turned to plunder and poverty.

Right after the Islamic Revolution, Fred immigrated to the United States with his family. Unfortunately, the shadow of the Islamic regime followed them through news coverage of the hostage crisis, war, or terrorism. Fred was reluctant to mention where they came from, but the arrival of their beautiful daughter, Melody, delighted them and brightened their horizon. In the 1980s, he earned a doctoral degree from the University of Washington in Seattle, and launched his academic career, initially at Penn State and then at Cal State. As a professor and dean, he was eager to make a meaningful contribution to his new country.

CHAPTER 1

The Start of a Close Friendship with the United States

A couple of years before I was born, the long US–Iran dance began in the Soviet Union embassy not too far from my parent's home. During this historic WW2 Tehran Conference in 1943, President Franklin Delano Roosevelt called Iran a "bridge to victory" for providing the Allied forces a critical supply route from Persian Gulf to the Soviet Union to support their existential fight against Nazi Germany. The US president called Iran an allied country, promised to protect its independence, and help develop its economy. After President Roosevelt returned to the United States, he sparked an enduring friendship between the two countries with his profound words in a thank-you letter to Mohammad Reza Pahlavi, the shah of Iran: "Iran has always occupied a warm spot in American hearts, more than ever now that we are brothers in arms."

It was in Tehran that Allied powers agreed to launch Operation Overlord—the invasion of Normandy on 6 June 1944, "D-Day" that started the liberation of northwest Europe. This eventually led to the Berlin Declaration that legally dissolved Nazi Germany in June 1945; the day that I was born in Tehran. My parents in Iran had experienced much hardship during the early 1940s as the country was gripped with a typhus epidemic. Mass starvation resulted in millions of deaths as most resources, including food, fuel, and transportation were used for the war. But I entered a world that seemed peaceful and in a country that was allied with the richest and most powerful country in the world: the United States of America.

My dad, Fazlullah, was 49 years old when I was born and had worked as a civil servant in the country's ministry of finance most of his life. He retired as the deputy treasurer in the ministry when I was around 11 years old. He had lived under the Qajar and Pahlavi monarchs and told many stories of military occupations by British and Russian forces during both World Wars I and II despite Iran's declared neutrality during both wars. He attended French schools in Tehran, Saint Louis and Alliance Francaise, was an avid consumer of political and international news, and a fan of the United States. Based on his experience working with Americans, he thought they had a pragmatic attitude toward problem-solving, and unlike colonial powers, were more willing than most advanced countries to see Iran as a partner and share their expertise in helping it to modernize and move toward a civil society.

My dad told me about the legacy of Morgan William Shuster at the ministry of finance. Shuster, an American civil servant and lawyer, was sent by US President William Taft to head a mission in response to the government of Iran's request for technical assistance during a short window of constitutional monarchy there around 1911. The government of Iran had reached out to America for help since both the British and Russian empires were supporting monarchical dictatorships and were actively against creating a parliament or any steps toward democracy in Iran. Iran's legislative body, Majlis, appointed Schuster as the treasurer-general of the country in 1911, shortly after the discovery of oil in Iran—the first in the Middle East. My dad said the people in the ministry knew Shuster as an honest man and a professional who worked hard to help the people of Iran. Unfortunately, only after a year on the job, Shuster was forced out by the Russians under the threat of armed intervention. When Shuster returned to the US, he recounted his Iran experience in his book, The Strangling of Persia, which he dedicated to the Iranian people. He wrote about his constant clashes with the British and Russian officials who, according to him, did not want the people of Iran to succeed.

My father often talked about his experience working under Dr. Arthur Millspaugh, an American economist who came to Iran twice to reorganize and modernize the Iran's entire ministry of finance; in mid-1920s during Reza Shah, the founder of Pahlavi dynasty, and again in early 1940s shortly after the shah had replaced his father, Reza Shah, as the king. Dad told me that Millspaugh worked hard to make Iran free of foreign debt and dominance but was unable to fix the county's culture of corruption and inefficient bureaucracy. Later, I learned that Millspaugh wrote three books about ethics in the government of Iran: The American Task in Persia; The Missions of Arthur C. Millspaugh to Iran, 1943-1945, and Americans in Persia.

My mother, Iran, a beautiful woman who was quite popular among our extended family and friends, was quite a bit younger than my dad; she was only 21 when she had me. She had strong social skills, a great sense of humor, and was a loving and caring mother. She was born to Hashem and Farah Moayedi in 1924 in Mashhad, a province of Khorasan located in the northwest of Iran. She was 12 when her entire family migrated to Tehran during the Great Depression in the mid-1930s. My mother was a modern and independent woman who loved music and Persian poetry; she often recited poetry by Rumi, Saadi, Hafez, and others who celebrated love, life, and wisdom. She was especially fond of Ferdowsi, whose "Book of Kings," an epic poem he wrote about one thousand years earlier, provided a mythological account of life in greater Iran before the Arab invasion of the sixth century. My mother picked my Iranian name, Freydun, from that book; it is the name of a mythical king and hero who was an icon of victory and justice. Like many Iranians, my mom believed Ferdowsi saved the Farsi language and literature after it was almost destroyed by Arab rule for over two hundred years.

Reza Khan Pahlavi, known as Reza Shah, became king in 1925 and the Pahlavi dynasty replaced the Qajar dynasty that had ruled Iran for 125 years. According to my dad, despite Iran's rich cultural heritage, when Reza Shah became the king, most Iranians were not able to read and write except for some Koranic verses and prayers. This was especially true in the rural areas, where Shia clerics wielded much power and were against Westernizing efforts of Reza Shah. The king was popular among a large portion of Iranian society who believed that he built the foundation of modern Iran by unifying an ethnically diverse society, constructing an urbanized modern nation with safe roads, bridges, and tunnels, as well the trans-Iranian railroad, hospitals, schools, an organized military, and many institutions necessary for running a secular government.

My mom's view was that Reza Shah was unable to modernize a culture that was vastly tribal and feudal; a large peasant population was indoctrinated by rural clerics and had been exploited for centuries by feudal landlords. It is well known in Iran that Reza Shah fought hard to build a secular government by removing the power of Shia clerics who'd had a profound influence in the government and society during a good part of the Qajar dynasty. In doing so, he banned all public religious expressions, including Islamic outfits for men and hijab for women, as well as the Muslim's obligatory beard.

To make an example of his anti-clerical policies of secularization, he picked Mashhad, where my grandparents, Farah and Hashem, lived at the time with their two sons and five daughters, including my mother. Mashhad is a most revered site for Shias, home to the shrine of Imam Reza, the eighth Shia leader after the prophet Mohammad. My grandma Farah told me that when Reza Shah ordered soldiers to take off women's hijabs in public, hundreds of women took refuge in the Goharshad Mosque. The mosque was on sacred ground and part of the sprawling shrine of Imam Reza, the highest Shia figure buried in Iran. Farah witnessed the soldiers entering the mosque, resulting in injury and death. My mother wasn't wearing a hijab, but my grandmother thought that prohibiting women from wearing the hijab was not just an anti-clerical act but also an invasion of personal privacy and cultural tradition. Banning the hijab left an indelible hatred among Shia clerics so that after the 1979 Islamic Revolution, they turned Reza Shah's mausoleum into a public bathroom.

My dad believed Reza Shah was hoping to free Iran from the domination and rivalry of the Soviet Russia and the British Empire. Most Iranians know about the repeated Russian invasion of Iran and annexing the country's vast territories in the north between the Caspian and Black seas in the nineteenth century, among other times. There are also stories about Britain exploiting Iranian oil in the south and controlling the country through the Anglo-Iranian Oil Company (AIOC) almost since 1909 when oil was discovered in Iran.

By most accounts, in Reza Shah's quest to make Iran independent of the British and Soviet rivalry in Iran, he made a grave mistake by reaching out to Hitler at the start of WWII. He was known to have praised the Aryan race and Hitler himself; in 1935 he changed the country's formal name from Persia to its cultural name, Iran, meaning the land of Aryans. Reza Shah had declared Iran a neutral county during World War II and refused to allow the Allied forces to send help from the Persian Gulf to the Soviets he hated. In 1941, my parents witnessed the invasions of the British from the south and the Russians from the north of Iran, forcing Reza Shah to abdicate in favor of his son Mohammad Reza, known as the shah. The Allied forces exiled Reza Shah to South Africa until his death in 1944.

I was two years old when my brother, Farrokh, was born; Farrokh turned out to be the quiet type and was rather thin. Every day, my mom gave him some type of fish oil. I tasted it once out of curiosity; it had the most offensive odor and awful taste, no wonder Farrokh hated fish for decades, even after he became a medical doctor in the United States. I was three years old when the midwife came to our house and my youngest brother, Farhad, was born. Farhad had eczema when he was a baby, and my mother regularly put some type of ointment on his face, which was always red. He was a little chubby and sweet, but hyperactive! Once, when he was a toddler, he disappeared. We searched everywhere and I finally saw two little feet sticking out of a cookie cylinder that was shaking in the pantry. Farhad was upside down holding onto a bunch of cookies for dear life.

Soon after Farhad was born, my dad, the chief accountant to the zarabkhaneh (imperial mint), was transferred to the outskirts of Tehran. The mint had coinage rights to all gold coins

of Iran, which mostly showed a portrait of the shah. We moved into a modern government house next to the mint with a very large, beautiful garden full of mature trees with purple flowers. I loved the creek that ran through the property. In summer, the whole family slept on our spacious terrace; it was so much fun to sleep outside under the bright stars and see the fleeting lights of meteors. My brothers and I loved our German shepherd, Gorgi, whose name meant "a little wolf" in Farsi. Sadly, one day when the front gate was open, Gorgi ran out to the street and was killed by a passing military truck. That was a traumatic experience for our family!

About forty years after Gorgi had died, my wife and I were living in Brea, California, when our teenagers Mike and Melody brought home a German shepherd-collie mix puppy that looked exactly like my old dog so we named him after Gorgi in his memory. Gorgi was a member of our family for 17 years before he passed. He was very gentle, especially with the young children of our extended family who visited us frequently. He would take me for a long walk every night until he got older and arthritis slowed him down too much.

*****

When I was about six years old, my mother woke me up early one morning, she was wearing a black dress and told me we were going to Reza Shah's funeral. He had died in exile about seven years earlier, and his mummified body had been kept in Egypt until they finally brought it back to Tehran. His son, the shah, had built a family mausoleum near the Shah Abdol-Azim shrine, the seventh-generation grandson of Imam Ali, whom the Shias believe was the true successor of the prophet Mohammad.

A government bus took us and many of my dad's colleagues to Toopkhaneh Square in Tehran, a major point along the funeral procession route. Soon we were all standing on the balcony of the old Tehran Municipality Palace where a life-size statue of the late Reza Shah on a horse caught my eyes; it was in the middle of the large square surrounded by government buildings. Traditional Iranian architecture featuring huge repetitive arches and tall columns dominated the four sides of the square. Topkhana Square was the most public place in Tehran where elaborate fireworks exploded during festivities, and where they used to hang ordinary criminals. On that day, thousands of people stood on the sidewalk to pay their final respects to a man who had done much to modernize Iran.

As the funeral procession was slowly approaching, I saw a black-draped vehicle that looked like a small strange-looking truck. I also saw a group of bearded men sitting inside a truck wearing Muslim caps, not turbans, and who were all holding a book in their hands. I heard the recitation of the holy Koran from a loudspeaker. It was ironic that a man who had fought the influence of Shia Islam during his life now was embracing it in death.

After the funeral of Reza Shah, his son, the shah, was probably at one of the weakest points of his reign. A movement to constrain his authority according to Iran's 1906 constitution was initiated. During a fleeting moment of constitutional monarchy in Iran in 1951, Dr. Mohammad Mossadegh, a popular prime minister who had the backing of a diverse political association called the National Front, managed to nationalize the Iranian oil industry against the wishes of the shah and the British government. Mossadegh was a liberal democrat, came from a prominent family, had a doctorate in law from the University of Neuchatel, Switzerland, and was an astute lawyer and shrewd politician. He was *Time* magazine's "Man of The Year" in 1951. It has been well documented that the British were encouraging President Harry Truman to oust Mossadegh with his weakness toward communists as a pretext.

In his book, *The Persian Puzzle*, Kenneth M. Pollack, a former CIA (Central Intelligence Agency) analyst and National Security Council Official, suggests that Truman was keen in resolving the issue since he felt the problem may create a rift between the Western alliance or that Iran might fall into the hands of the Soviet Union. In an effort to resolve the conflict, Truman invited Mossadegh to the United States in 1951 and discussed the issue, apparently without success. In the meantime, the extraction, refining, and selling of Iranian oil halted, creating an economic disaster in Iran. Based on the media reports, the weakening of Mossadegh came about as a result of poor economic conditions and his liberal views that clashed with his key supporter, Ayatollah Kashani, the speaker of parliament and political voice of the conservative Shia clerics at the time. Pollack suggest that the British were taking advantage of the situation by sending money to the opposition's parliamentarians and newspapers to widen the cracks among Mossadegh supporters.

Around 1952, my dad was transferred from the imperial mint back to the headquarters of the ministry of finance in Tehran. He later mentioned that due to the lack of oil revenue and the economic downturn in the country, the mint had little activity, not to mention there was not much appetite to issue more gold coins portraying Mohammad Reza Pahlavi under the Mossadegh government.

We moved into a new house in Tehran that our dad had built on a lot available to senior civil servants at a discount. It was a large corner house built with steel beams, cement, and bricks that had six rooms, a large kitchen, and a nice balcony accessed from the second floor and from the backyard by a staircase on which my mother placed a large geranium in a vase on the right side of each step. Most importantly, the house had a small pool where my brothers and I taught ourselves how to swim. We had a couple of basements that were quite cool during summertime, a luxury, since most people did not have fans, let alone air conditioning to fight Tehran's dry and hot summers.

The house had an internal piping network for water, but the capital city still had to wait a few years before it had a water supply network. Drinking water was delivered every morning in yellow water tanks on a horse-driven carriage. We kept water from the creek in our *abanbar* (water storage), which you could find in every house. The water storage, below the basement, was the coldest place in the house and in the room next to it, we kept ice and fruits.

Most fruits and vegetables were delivered daily to the house by vendors who used donkeys or carts for transportation and knew what all the housewives on our street wanted. Milk was delivered in late afternoons by a milkman wearing an old fedora who carried two containers on the back of his bike with a loud rubber ball squeeze air horn that was the same for all milkmen. My mom bought meat or poultry, vegetables and eggs every day. The grocer, Mr. Aghajani, wore a gray uniform and personally inspected every egg by passing a light through them to make sure they were good. Most people had an account with the grocer, although he had a sign on his wall saying something like: "I don't sell on credit since I would like to see you again." He was the richest man in the neighborhood, but ironically, he had the lowest social status as a grocer.

We lived close to my uncle, Fatollah, and his two sons, Cameran and Cyrus. My uncle's wife, Bejee, took advantage of the emancipation of women during the Pahlavi rule and became a role model for women's fashion within the family and beyond. She was an independent and an avant-garde woman who created a magazine called *Bejee*. She divorced my uncle and later emigrated to the US where she opened a successful boutique. My uncle was an army veterinarian and a one-star general who was close to my dad. His son, Cyrus, had several beautiful pigeons and was often on the roof flying them. I was always surprised that they all came back in the evening and went into the nest that Cyrus had made for them with bamboo cane. There was a pigeon shop in our neighborhood where he and some of the other kids his age bought or exchanged pigeons. My favorite was a fantail white pigeon with one blue and one gray eye. Cyrus was quite talented with his hands and made a nice sail ship with ice cream sticks. My uncle had always dogs that were close to the Pomeranian breed and named Tommy, Jolly, and such.

In August 1953, I was eight years old and in a taxicab returning from a shopping trip with my mother in Toopkhaneh Square when we saw a mob lowering the Reza Shah's large statue from its pedestal by ropes. This was the statue of him on horseback that had caught my eye during his funeral a couple of years earlier. My mother and I were shocked. The driver was telling my

21

mom that the shah had fled Iran after trying unsuccessfully to fire his prime minister, Mossadegh; later we saw riots everywhere and people chanting "Long live Mossadegh!"

A week or so later, my uncle and my dad were glued to the radio instead of reading the daily newspaper as they usually did. There was much commotion on the street; hundreds of people were standing on top of moving buses and trucks. Taxis and private cars had their lights on and were waving the Iranian flag! In contrast to the events several days earlier, they were holding a picture of the shah in his military uniform with all his many medals. Some had put his picture on the front windshield of their cars. My uncle's housekeeper who was a soldier got on one of the buses but was returned to the same spot; it was like a hop-on hop-off ride. I asked him to take me but he was not allowed to. My dad mentioned that these were the same street thugs who had brought down the statues of the shah and his father around Tehran a couple of weeks earlier, but now they were chanting "Long live the shah!" My dad told my uncle that General Zahedi, the new prime minister, was making a speech on the radio. The program was followed by military music.

Based on media reports, when President Eisenhower was elected to office, he decided to go along with the British and remove Mossadegh. Eisenhower feared the communist Soviet Union would control the vast oil resources of Iran and obtain access to the Persian Gulf so he joined the British in ousting Mossadegh. The coup initially failed and the shah fled to Italy around the time my mother and I saw mobs bringing down his father's statue.

I heard on the radio that the mob had invaded Mossadegh's home and looted all his belongings in an operation called AJAX. Based on press reports, Kermit Roosevelt, an American intelligence officer and the grandson of President Theodore Roosevelt, engineered the coup under the direction of Allen Dulles, the director of the United States CIA, in collaboration with its British counterpart, MI6. Mossadegh was arrested, imprisoned, and later was put under house arrest in his residence in Ahmadabad. He died there in 1967 when I was in college in the United States. I heard he was denied a funeral and was buried in his dining room.

My uncle, a general, was convinced that Iran was about to become a communist country since Mossadegh was weak and communists had infiltrated the military. After the coup, many military officers were convicted of being members of the communist party Tudeh; most were executed by a firing squad. People often had stories about an officer in their family who was either executed or sentenced to long prison terms by the military tribunals.

My dad said that about a year after the fall of the Mossadegh government, the shah agreed to the creation of a 25-year international oil consortium where US and British companies owned 40 percent of Iran's oil and the Dutch and French owned 20 percent. The oil was flowing again—albeit production, refining, transportation, and marketing was done by Westerners since Iran lacked the necessary expertise, resources, and connections. Nevertheless, my dad thought the revenue was helping the shah to pay for part of his agenda of modernization and Westernization of Iran.

*****

After the 1953 coup, the shah's regime and Iran itself became much stronger and a closer ally of the United States. Having the strong backing of the US, the shah's focus was on subtly weaken religion's influence on the government to advance his White Revolution agenda of secularizing and modernizing Iran. Communist organizations were crushed and many militant clerics were arrested, but there was still the underground Shia organization Fedayeen of Islam that had been created in 1946 by Navab Safavi. A theology student, Safavi sought to transform Iran into an Islamic country run by a Shia jurisprudent and to purify the country from corruption and foreign influence through targeted assassinations. In 1946, the group assassinated Ahmad Kasrvai, an outspoken critic of Shia clerics, while he was being tried for "slander of Islam." It also assassinated two pro-Western prime ministers: Abdolhassein Hazhir in 1949 and Ali Razmara in 1951. Evading arrest and punishment until 1955 after a failed assassination of Hossein Ala, another prime minister of Iran; Safavi was arrested and executed, thanks to the shah's newly found power and the apparent disappearance of Shia clerics from Iran's political scene in 1953. According to some clerics, Navab Safavi was an inspiration for the concept of *Wilayat e Faghih*, or guardianship of Islamist jurist; he has been revered by the Islamic Republic, and the Fedayeen of Islam became a legal political party in Iran about a year after the Islamic Revolution.

As a sign of increasing the US–Iran friendship, the shah invited Vice President Richard Nixon for a visit in December of 1953. Relations with the US became stronger, and around 1962, when I was in high school, Iranian media reported the shah's official state visit to the United States at the invitation of President John F. Kennedy and his wife; the shah delivered a speech before a joint meeting of the US Congress.

After 1953, we gradually began to see more American people in Iran as well as American movies, songs, and other cultural products. The shah embraced Western values and cultures and as a result, travel between the two countries gradually expanded; high school students were exposed to the English language as part of their curriculum and private English classes were widely available by the time I was in high school. America was a huge attraction and most of my high school classmates were dreaming of going to the United States after graduation to study. It seemed the economy was improving and people's lifestyle was changing. Unlike their mothers, young urban women—including my mom and aunts and their friends—were not wearing a hijab. My dad and his colleagues wore suits and ties.

Our parents took us to many fun places. My mom's favorite place, the Café Continental, had a courtyard full of beautiful pomegranate trees; we loved their automatic ice cream dispensers, which were quite new in those days. We also used to visit the two amusement parks in Tehran: The Boat Club and Café Shahrdari or Municipality Café. The Boat Club had a large pond with small motorboats operated by staff wearing sailor uniforms; we loved their Ferris wheel. Café Shahrdari had a nice merry-go-round where I could see my dad's joy as he watched us go round and round on horses and other animals. They also had a long puppet show; we loved it when the puppet got mad and squirted water on us. Our parents bought us ice cream, potato chips, cotton candy and, eventually, mortadella sandwiches with pickles, butter, and tomato. Those sandwiches tasted great!

My mother loved restaurants with live bands. Two outdoor cafes in the suburb of Tehran, Tajrish, each in one of the two main squares, were located at the foot of the Alborz Mountain range. One was Café Jahan, the other was Café Astara. Both had live music and dinner, women in Turkish costume sang beautiful songs on a stage in the garden. By the end of the long show, it was cold, and we kids were all asleep on our chairs.

As the country's economy improved, we traveled to quite a few cities, especially during Nowruz, Nowruz has been celebrated for centuries and literally means a new day. It is the beginning of the first day of the Farsi calendar and the first day of spring equinox, around March 21. Spring equinox is when the sun crosses the celestial equator and the night and day are the same length. So, the Iranian new year begins at the same moment around the world. Once we went with our extended maternal family to Shiraz. My maternal uncle Mohsen was appointed as the head of the Fars Province Endowment Foundation, Oghaf, and lived in a suburb of Shiraz, about 560 miles south of Tehran. He invited the entire family to visit him during the 1954 Nowruz holidays. Three generations traveled together, including my mom and dad, my two brothers, my mother's four sisters and brother, their spouses, and our cousins. We all laughed and screamed when the bus bounced over many ups and downs on the road. We felt like we were in a race and cheered for our driver as he overtook a bus from another company, which happened many times during the long trip. It was a two-day trip and we all stayed overnight in a hotel in the City of Esfahan.

Next to my uncle's house in Shiraz, there was a field full of beautiful red tulips. I felt free and happy running in the field as though I was going to fly! During our stay in Shiraz, we visited the mausoleums of Saadi and Hafez, two beloved Iranian poets of the thirteenth and fourteenth centuries. Like most Iranians, my mom kept her poetry books close and often cited the verses in lieu of advice. We also visited Persepolis, the capital of Achaemenid Empire from 550 to 330 BC. It is in Marvdasht outside of Shiraz. The architecture and many ancient artifacts and arts definitely spoke of a powerful country with a great artistic and engineering capability. Persepolis allows Iranians to bask in the past glory and feel a sense of pride; I was no exception, albeit very young.

During one of the Nowruz holidays, we visited the beautiful city of Isfahan, which was the capital of Seljuq around the eleventh century; it was also the capital during the Safavid dynasty that ruled the country around the sixteenth and part of seventeenth centuries referred to as the golden age. The Safavids made Shia Islam the official religion although there were Shia communities inside and outside of Iran before that. The Safavid revitalized and glorified it through magnificent arts and architecture. Most Iranians were converted to Shia Islam during the Safavid reign. We visited Sheikh Lutfullah and Masjid-e-Emam mosques, among the masterpieces of architecture and tile work of the Safavid era. We also saw the Si-o-se-pol or the bridge of 33, the largest of the 11 bridges on the Zayanderud, the largest river of the Iranian Plateau.

Among my childhood travels during Nowruz holidays was Abadan in the oil-rich province of Khuzestan about six hundred miles south of Tehran. It housed the largest oil refinery in the world and the modern-looking city had been built by the British. The small towns and villages along the way had traditional buildings but the religious population was scant. In Abadan, I learned about the separatist movement of the oil-rich Khuzestan province under the leadership of Sheikh Khazal and his rebellious Arab forces who established an independent Sheikdom from 1922 to 1924, which was abolished by Reza Shah.

The shah had successfully removed the influence of Shia clerics from the educational experience of my generation by adopting a Western model controlled by the government. But religion was still an important factor among most Iranians. In 1955, my fourth-grade teacher, Mr. Naderi, a clean-shaven young man with glasses who usually wore a white shirt and tie, gave us an assignment that entailed researching and writing a short essay about one of the five principles of Shia Islam with the help of our parents; my assigned topic was "justice." We were required to present our findings in class. I asked my grandpa, Hashem—who had a great sense of humor and was quite knowledgeable—to help me write a short essay about the significance of justice. I loved the final work and memorized it in its entirety. I practiced every day and presented my little essay from memory in class. It went quite well; my classmates spontaneously applauded and the teacher seemed to be quite impressed.

Soon after I returned to my seat, a group of heavyset men, including our principal who had a big mustache and curly hair, entered our classroom. We all stood in respect as was customary. The men accompanying the principal were inspectors from the ministry of education. The principal asked if anyone had learned the lesson that Mr. Naderi had given that day. His tone of voice was authoritative and intimidating so there was a deafening silence in class. Everyone was too scared to say anything. I could see fear and embarrassment in the teacher's eyes as he looked at me. Finally, he asked me to give my presentation once more for our guests. I got up and stood by the board but could not utter a word of my presentation. Somehow, it had escaped my mind. The class was so quiet that you could hear a pin drop. Mr. Naderi's face was white as chalk. I finally remembered a few bits and pieces from my presentation then added a few things and saved the day. I could see relief on the face of Mr. Naderi and our principal.

By the time I was in the fifth grade, the shah dominated everything. We had to stand in movie theaters when they played the national anthem that strongly featured the shah in the lyrics and in the visuals. At school, we had to pray for his health every morning. The shah's birthday was an important national holiday, upstaging most, if not all, religious celebrations. In the beginning fifth grade, I was selected along with my cousin, Cameran, and hundreds of other students from all over Tehran to participate in a special show to be performed live on October 26, 1957, in front of the shah on his 38th birthday. It would be in Amjadieh Stadium, the largest in Iran at the time with the capacity of thirty thousand people. Most families listened to the annual event broadcast on Radio Iran. Our show consisted of students who covered the entire soccer field, moving in formation with music to create colorful geometric shapes with our props. I believe we also created the image of a royal crown. We practiced very hard on a dirt field in the school yard for a couple of weeks and then were bussed daily to the stadium to join other students in practicing on a grass field with music playing. We were happy to be out of school for weeks and it felt so nice to practice on grass; it smelled nice and fresh. We performed flawlessly in front of the shah and the spectators applauded for a long time! It was a smashing success, aside from the political aspects.

I loved the sound of band music that we heard during our practice and wanted to play the trumpet. For sixth grade, I went to a new school with my brothers and, for the first time ever, we had a music class as most schools did not offer a music class due to lack of teachers. Our teacher was an old man who played a violin and asked students to sing patriotic songs in class. He encouraged us to ask our parents to buy a musical instrument so we could practice. On several occasions, I asked my dad to buy me a trumpet but he told me it was not a good idea since blowing into the instrument too much could result in a hernia. To date, I am not sure if his advice was related to health or purely financial. So, I never got a chance to play a wind instrument as I had wished. However, I learned to whistle parts of popular songs over the years and created my own songs by whistling.

In Iran, high school started in the seventh grade. One of my most exciting memories was when we visited the school laboratory where the teacher demonstrated how a car's transmission and clutch worked. I was fascinated by the mechanism in action and was looking forward to another visit but that never happened. By the eighth grade, I was happy to ride my bike to school although I had to navigate in chaotic Tehran traffic.

There were still several political parties when I was in the ninth grade, and the shah's White Revolution and relationship with the United States was not fully supported by all quarters. One day in 1961, we students all received a letter asking us to show up in front of the parliament building (Majlis) in Baharestan Square in Tehran on a certain day. The letter asked us to copy it 10 times and distribute it to our friends. The message protested increasing the passing grade from seven to 12 on a scale of one to 20. But in essence, it was a political rally against the shah using teachers' salaries and students' grades as an excuse.

Thousands of students and teachers gathered in front of the parliament building. A speaker was complaining about rampant corruption in the country and total surrender to a foreign power. Later, I heard Khanali, one of the speakers at the demonstration, was killed by a police officer. On our way back to school, our demonstration devolved into chanting slogans like "I need a wife, now!" I believe the change in the passing grade was temporarily rescinded.

I started wrestling during ninth grade. It was a popular sport in Iran; world champions like Gholamreza Takhti, Imam Ali Habibi, Mansour Mehdizadeh, and others were celebrities in Iran at that time. Close to our school, the sports club Bashgah Kian had equipment for bodybuilding, weightlifting, a very coarse wrestling mat, and a makeshift shower. A sign on the wall close to the wrestling mat said, "Defeat is the introduction to victory." I have shared that line with my children and grandchildren when they had a setback in a game or at school. Bodybuilding was mostly for blue collar workers. My friends and I occasionally went there during lunchtime to wrestle. One day after a few rounds of warmups, my friend pulled a strong half nelson on me and dislocated my shoulder. The next morning, my mom took me to a guy in *Hasan Abad Circle* in downtown Tehran. The man was not a doctor, but he had a great reputation for healing my type of injury. He asked me to look up to see a pigeon, and as soon as I did, he made a move that put my shoulder back in place. He then wrapped some ash, egg, date, and lamb fat around

31

my shoulder. I was good after a couple of weeks. But I never went back to wrestling.

Around 1961, we moved to our new home in the north of Tehran, a more affluent area on Roosevelt Avenue. The new house had three floors, each like a complete apartment. Soon we made many new friends; my uncle's house was next door and we were still close to my cousins Cameran and Cyrus, who both went to the United States after high school. We picked vacant land close to our house and created a decent soccer field with wooden gates, albeit on dirt. A man who lived next to our field that didn't have young children voluntarily watered our field every day before we started playing and sometimes it got muddy. We played every afternoon during summer and weekends and formed a neighborhood team to play against other teams, but most of the time, we played for money.

Something magical happened during the first day of 10th grade at my new school. Our classroom was on the second floor of a traditional Iranian building. There were several long Palladian arch windows on one side of the classroom and a solid wall on the other side. I was on the window side watching a basketball game in the courtyard below when our young, well-dressed English teacher walked into the classroom and immediately turned to us who were sitting on the window side to ask if we were enjoying the game. He then asked the other group if they were enjoying the wall since they had no window to see anything. He told us that the English language is like a window to the world that could help us experience new cultures, meet new people, and better enjoy their food, art, movies, and music. Until then, I had felt English class was boring, but the little talk turned on the proverbial light bulb in my head!

That evening, my mother agreed to let me enroll in an after-school English class. The owner, Mr. Shokouh, was a businessman and had predicted the rising demand for learning English as the shah's White Revolution and modernizing efforts brought Iran closer to the West, especially to the United States. The classes were held in a modern learning center and they were co-ed, something that I had not experienced since first grade. Initially, Mr. Shokouh showed us how to construct simple sentences by putting the subject first, then the verb, and finally, the object. He also demonstrated the role of vowels in English by striking the bottom of his shoe to the floor.

Several weeks later we watched the 1959 movie *A Summer Place*, a romantic drama with Sandra Dee and Troy Donohue in its original language. I did not understand much of the dialogue, but loved the theme music, the romance, and the breathtaking scenery, which later I learned was filmed in California. That's when I fell in love with America and American English, perhaps naively and for the wrong reasons. I attended English classes in the Iran-American Society and kept a small English dictionary in my pocket literally everywhere I went. I also listened to the American Armed Forces Radio as the only audio resource available at home, although most subjects were irrelevant to me. I saw American movies in their original languages on Monday nights at 10 p.m. in the Moulin Rouge movie theater on Old Shemiran Road, about a 40-minute walk from our house on Roosevelt Ave. Sometimes on the way back, I would take a shortcut through vacant lots and encounter packs of vicious street dogs, some possibly infected with rabies, but that could not stop me from going.

One early morning in June 1962 a year before I graduated from high school, I was enjoying the view of the beautiful turquoise water of the sprawling Karaj Dam as our bus traveled north on the scenic Chalus Road. I had just completed my 11th grade final exams and was so excited to get away from the hot and boring summer of Tehran. I was going to spend time with my cousins who lived in Noshahr, a quiet resort town with pristine beaches and deep green forests on the southern coast of the Caspian Sea. I loved the Caspian region and was sad that it would be my last visit before I went to America to attend college. We passed gorgeous waterfalls and springs, wound through valleys and numerous bridges and tunnels and as soon as we exited the long Kandovan Tunnel on the other side of the Alborz Mountain range, I felt the cool and pleasant breeze. The beautiful natural surroundings and scenery felt worlds away from the congested urban environment of Tehran. A few hours later, the fresh fragrance of rice paddies welcomed us to the Caspian region.

The Caspian Sea is the largest inland body of water in the world with about 450 miles of scenic coastline in the Northern Iranian provinces of Gilan and Mazandaran; back then, the old Soviet Union shared the rest of the coastline. We heard very little in school or in the media about our mysterious northern neighbors; people were afraid to even mention Russia. The shah, a staunch ally of the United States, and like most Iranians, saw the Soviet Union as an existential threat to Iran's sovereignty.

The driver dropped me off at my aunt's home in Noshahr. Aunt Shokouh was a few years younger than my mother, who was the oldest among her four sisters. Shokouh's husband, Reza, was the city's chief of police. That afternoon, we all went swimming in the Caspian Sea. My cousin and I went so far that we could hardly see the shore. I wondered how Russia looked and whether anyone could swim all the way there.

The port of Noshahr had been built about 30 years earlier by the shah's father, Reza Shah Pahlavi, but in 1962 with no maritime activities, it was quiet. That suddenly changed when the shah and his wife, Empress Farah, arrived. The shah's imperial guardsmen had come earlier by trucks and buses and camped across from my aunt's house. The off-duty guards played serious volleyball all day long. Some of the shah's entourage stayed in the shah's villa next to my aunt's house, which was surrounded by a large garden full of beautiful citrus trees. The shah's ship was anchored in the middle of the sapphire blue water of the port's harbor. I could see *Shahsavar* on the portside in decorative Farsi calligraphy. The royals occasionally flew to Noshahr during summer for a few days of relaxation. Over the next couple of days, I saw them water ski in the harbor with the vibrant Caspian Sea in the background. Waterskiing was a new phenomenon in Iran, and I had never seen anyone do it. The shah was not only ahead of the country in water sports, but also his grand vision for modernizing Iran was hardly understood by most Iranians. He was about to embark on an ambitious political, economic, and social reform plan known as the White Revolution, promising to urbanize and industrialize Iran and provide equal rights for women in our highly religious and rural country.

The shah had crushed both liberals and communists after the 1953 coup when he ousted Mossadegh, but then was facing a formidable alliance of powerful landowners who were fiercely resisting giving up their farmlands and Shia clerics who were vehemently against westernizing Iran. In 1961, the shah dissolved Majlis, the Iranian legislative body, and passed his controversial land-reform law, in which large landowners were forced to sell their tract of farmland to their cultivators and received stocks of state-owned industrial companies in return. The rural cooperatives replaced the financial support of the landowners.

About 55 miles west of Noshahr was the magnificent Hotel Ramsar, my favorite spot on the shores of the Caspian Sea. It was also built by Reza Shah in the early 1930s in the Mazandaran province where he was originally from. The hotel was located on a green hill with a mile-long tree-lined boulevard in front leading to the Caspian Sea in the city of Ramsar. The hotel's art deco architecture certainly conveyed modernism and a European taste. Another legacy of Reza Shah was the old Chalus Hotel several miles away from my aunt's home. It was a fun bike ride to pass by endless rice fields with beautiful, lush mountain forests in the background. The hotel was part of the Pahlavi Foundation and a legacy of Reza Shah. The hotel menu listed Western cuisines like beef stroganoff and schnitzel along with Caspian Sea white fish. My cousin and I would order the least expensive item in the menu: crème caramel. We loved it.

That summer, I saw ample signs of American art, entertainment, and culture in Noshahr. In the evenings, we hung out in a café called Plage. It was built on an elevated wooden platform right on the beach. They served hamburgers, chicken sandwiches, soft drinks, beer, and other alcoholic beverages with a limited choice of Iranian cuisines. The place was full of suntanned men plus women in bikinis. For the first time, I saw an American coin-operated jukebox that had buttons with letters on them. We listened to Paul Anka's "You Are My Destiny," and "Put Your Head on My Shoulder." They were so romantic and the words were simple and easy to understand. There were other songs we heard on the jukebox like Ray Charles' "Hit the Road, Jack" and Elvis Presley's "Jailhouse Rock," although it was not easy to understand the lyrics.

The younger people played nascent Iranian pop and jazz music as opposed to the Iranian classical genre that was rather poetic, subdued, and which appealed more to the older generation. Iranian pop and jazz icon Vigen was popular among the young middle-class, while female singers like Delkash and Marzieh were household names. The Mazandarani and many other types of folkloric music and dances were local phenomena and quite popular among the small town and rural population. Empress Farah had a vision of supporting the preservation of Iran's diverse local cultures, including folkloric music and dances, by giving them national exposure through numerous festivals and media events.

The vast majority of Iranians were still waiting to experience modern life, though. The only gas station in Noshahr was an old American Oil hand-crank gas pump located in Rajabi Kerosene shop in a residential area, only accessible through a labyrinth of narrow dirt alleys where people lived in small quarters without proper sanitation. Every time I was there, I saw local women carrying spring water while holding the hands of their small children, some of whom were not wearing shoes. Rural women seemed to be quite busy taking care of family and working in the fields. Most regular policemen, including my uncle's driver, lived there in dilapidated homes. The police department accountant, a local, lived with a family of five in a two-room newer government house that was elevated about 10 feet from the ground—like most homes—because of high humidity and mud. We heard that the floor collapsed on the wedding night of his younger daughter, resulting in the bride, groom, and their bed falling through all the way to the ground, but fortunately, there were no injuries. The whole town was talking about how the wooden structures had rotted after decades of exposure to high humidity since Reza Shah built the entire town in 1935.

One of the legacies of Reza Shah was the centralization of the government by sending men from Tehran to run the police department, health office, post and telegraph offices, the national bank branch, gendarmerie (military police) and the port, among other organizations. In Noshahr, these men had a regular card game on Thursday nights when the weekend started in Iran. American and European card games like poker and rummy were replacing popular Iranian family games of pasur and hokm among the elites. These men played a five-card draw poker game with the buy-in of about $15; in a typical night, the equivalent of several hundred US dollars changed hands. The ladies, including my Aunt Shokouh, played 13-card rummy for money and ended their game around midnight; the men played until about 4 a.m. since Fridays were holidays. Men drank scotch, vodka, and beer while the women mainly had soft drinks and tea. My uncle allowed me and my cousin, Shahram, to sit behind him to watch how he played all night. Sometimes the other players could read his bluff by looking at our surprised, worried faces.

One evening, I witnessed the entry of an original American invention into the entertainment scene in Iran during the last week of my stay in Noshahr in the summer of 1962. I saw a large crowd gathered around what they called the jackpot. It was a coin-operated slot machine displaying fruits like lemons, plums, and cherries as well as liberty bells. It took one 5-Rial coin, which was slightly more than a nickel. It paid out 18 coins if the three bells lined up, and a lot more if the three jackpot icons lined up. Everyone was so excited and cheered whenever the machine paid out. People were waiting in a long line for their turn to play. During the next couple of days, many beach employees, restaurant workers, and countless visitors lost quite a bit of money in the slot machine. The angry crowd was threatening to break apart the machine to take their money out. Uncle Reza ordered the slot machine to be secured until the issues were resolved. A police sergeant placed it in the jailhouse where the problem got much worse; during the next few days, policemen and prisoners lost a great deal of their money to the machine.

The slot machine and the beach café belonged to the vast Pahlavi Foundation; a charity organization used by the shah. The Foundation owned hotels, casinos, and many other properties along the Caspian shores and elsewhere in the country. My uncle was ordered to put the slot machine back into the Plage and have it protected. One late night when we went with Reza to check on the slot machine, we were shocked to see the sergeant in charge of protecting the machine completely drunk; he'd tossed his police jacket onto a chair and was frantically putting one coin after the other into the slot machine while a few café guests waited for their turn. It was funny to see how fast he sobered up and stood at attention when he saw his boss, Reza. He was sent to jail for a week or so. Apparently, he liked his alcohol.

We ran into the sergeant again in Noshahr right after the Islamic Revolution about 17 years later. Earlier that day, we celebrated Iranian New Year in my cousin's villa in Noshahr. My uncle had retired as a police colonel, but we jokingly asked him to find us some wine in his old city; surprisingly, Reza agreed and we ventured into town. After a short drive, we arrived at police headquarters where my uncle worked in the early 1960s. It was guarded by many young men with heavy beards wearing looted camouflage military jackets and holding machine guns who were sitting behind sandbags. Occasionally, the revolutionaries brought in someone whose eyes were covered and sometimes, their hands were tied too; a purge of the city was well underway. Reza spotted the old sergeant who had been in charge of the slot machine. He was retired too, in civilian clothing sporting a heavy beard and standing close to the old police building. My uncle and the retired sergeant had a short conversation and we soon were following his small car on a curvy narrow side road for about 10 minutes. We stopped at an old house where Reza went inside and shortly after emerged with a sack full of exquisite French wine. The Islamic revolutionaries had raided the shah's villa next to my aunt's old house a few days before; they broke empty bottles in front of a crowd and chanted "God is great!" in Arabic. The expensive wines from the shah's cellar, however, had found their way onto the black market. We had a great time and celebrated Nowruz with his imperial majesty's wine that evening.

For 12th grade, I joined my brothers at Adib High School on Lalezar Avenue next to Kayhan, the largest newspaper in Iran, where one of my friends was a typesetter. As part of the high school curriculum, we had a class called Fiqh that covered Islamic jurisprudence. A clergyman taught it by telling boring stories. We always envied our Christian, Armenian, Jewish, or Zoroastrian classmates who were exempt from attending that class and allowed to go out and play. We were told the religion of most Iranians before the Muslim conquest during the seventh century was Zoroastrian, but during the two centuries of Arab rule, most Iranians converted to Sunni Islam. In the sixteenth century, the Safavid dynasty made Shia Islam the official religion of Iran. Some believe it was done to unify the country against the powerful Sunni Ottoman rivals in the west of Iran, while others held the Safavid genuinely believed in Shia Islam and had great disdain for the Sunnis.

Our religious study teacher was a short man with a large turban and glasses who students loved to make fun of. The class furniture was the same during all the years I went to school. It consisted of benches and long tables in front of each bench, one after the other in two columns. One day, he announced with excitement that he just passed his driver's license test. Just the thought of a short guy like him in his turban and robe driving a car seemed so funny! After hearing the news, the class erupted in laughter. Soon, everyone stood atop the long wooden tables and chanted something like "Bravo!" Students shredded paper and threw it out of the second-floor window to the street as confetti. We were all laughing and having a great time until the stern-looking principal who scared the daylight out of everyone showed up and sent a few students home.

Right after my high school final exams, precisely on my 18th birthday in 1963, Ayatollah Khomeini—an outspoken critic of the shah's policies, especially his White Revolution—inspired a major demonstration in Tehran. This was just a couple of years after the massive demonstration of teachers and students in Tehran. The protest was crushed and Tayeb Haj Rezae, the street leader of the protest, was arrested. My old neighbor, General Shayanfar, was his government-appointed lawyer. He told me he felt the verdict had already been determined before the trial even began; Tayeb Haj Rezae was executed. Ayatollah Khomeini was arrested and exiled after a year in prison. He spent most of his time in exile in Najaf, Iraq, which is considered the third holiest city of Shia Islam. There in Najaf, he developed his idea of the *Valayat-e-Fakeeh*, or the Governance of Jurist, which ultimately resulted in the creation of the Islamic Republic of Iran. While Khomeini was living in exile, his anti-shah fellow clerics and supporters of the 1963 uprising were serving long-term prison sentences and few people were aware of their existence. I was focused on going to America and tuned out everything else.

After my high school graduation, my dad was determined to help me to go to the United States despite the enormous cost involved. I needed a passport and an acceptance from a US university to get a student visa. Getting a passport was not an easy matter. First, I had to get an invitation from someone who lived abroad and was established, then I had to obtain clearance from our local police station before I could go to the passport office to fill out the application in person. It took several months to put all the paperwork together. Later, I heard from my mom that my dad had sold his only parcel of land, his entire savings, to finance my trip.

In the early 1960s, an organization in Tehran called American Friends of the Middle East (AFME) helped students to get into US universities. They provided information and assisted in obtaining the I-20 form required by the American consulate to issue student visas. The organization was run by Mr. Ziegler, who had blond hair and spoke some Farsi. I frequently visited the office, albeit with no tangible results. I think the organization might have figured out that I did not have enough funds.

Finally, I was fed up with all the waiting and, against the advice of my friends, decided to go for a tourist visa instead. It was a long shot to obtain a US tourist visa, given my age, and having visited the AFME would certainly indicate that I was not going there as a tourist, but to study. However, my dad agreed to go with me to the US consulate in Tehran.

The consulate was not crowded; I guess few people could afford to visit the United States in 1964. I was impressed by the pretty and polite secretaries and the nicely carpeted rooms. After a brief wait, we were called in for the interview. The consul was a young man who spoke some Farsi in a thick accent. The first question he asked was why I did not wait to get an acceptance through the AFME office. It was impossible to keep up my pretense as a tourist so I told the truth: they were too slow. He seemed to like my response but in a friendly tone said that to study in the US, I needed to get an acceptance from a university there.

I told him honestly that I was thinking of going to aviation school to become a pilot. My dad was shocked to hear that since most Iranian dads wanted their sons to be either a doctor or an engineer. Before letting us utter another word, the consul gave me an unlimited multiple-entry US tourist visa; I was ecstatic. It was one of the best moments of my life.

The next day, my dad and I went to buy an airline ticket. I wanted to stay overnight in London so that I could see my Aunt Noushi, who I missed and who was about my age even though the stop complicated the itinerary. After buying an Air France ticket, we took the bus to an exchange shop on Manouchehri Avenue in Tehran where my father bought $700 worth of travelers checks on the black market since there were restrictions for foreign currency exchange in Iran. It was quite a bit of money, but my dad was under the impression that this was seed money— I would work in the US and take care of my expenses as many others had done.

Now, I have the visa, the air ticket, and the US dollars. As greetings and farewells are important signs of respect and friendship in the Iranian culture, some of our closer family members stayed in our house the night before my departure. The rest, including my best friends, came the next day and gave me presents. One of the best presents was a Phillips electric shaver that saved me from frequently cutting my face with cheap blades. I also got an imitation Mont Blanc pen which I loved, a leather wallet and a few nice shirts.

My mom gave me two handmade, extra-thick woolen pullover sweaters since she had heard that February was quite cold on the East Coast. She had woven them with two metal sticks as many women did those days in Iran. Unfortunately, I got too hot whenever I wore them indoors in the US.

After breakfast, we all headed to Tehran Mehrabad International Airport, which had only one terminal. We had gone there so many times over the years to see off or greet family members. I loved to watch the large airplanes landing or taking off, especially at night. I also enjoyed hearing announcements in several languages. After I checked in my heavy luggage at the counter, they told me that I should wait for the announcement. Apparently, they did make the announcement, but I was busy talking with my friends and taking pictures while my mom went all-out in showing her warm hospitality to our family and friends by offering them fruits and snacks. We never heard the announcement. After a couple of hours of not hearing about my flight, I went and checked at the counter, where to my extreme surprise and dismay, I was told my flight had left about an hour ago.

How could it leave without me? They told me there was an EL AL flight just leaving, and I could catch it if I ran. It was a chaotic situation; as I was running toward the plane, everyone gathered on the airport balcony to see me off and I could hear my friends and brothers shouting my name repeatedly—it was such an endearing gesture of sincerity and I loved it so much. I still feel their genuine warmth and love. My luggage was sitting next to the aircraft like everyone else's since they only put it on the plane when a passenger identified his or her luggage for security reasons. I started climbing the stairs to board the plane, wearing my thick overcoat and holding a heavy, overstuffed carry-on sack. Soon after I got in, the door slammed shut and the plane was starting to taxi. I had no idea what I was supposed to do. As the plane started to take off, one of the flight attendants saw my face and moved me to sit next to an older gentleman.

I was concerned about whether I could study in America with my tourist visa. The service was great, and after a while, I started a conversation with the gentleman sitting next to me. He was a businessman from Israel who was going home. Up until 1979, Iran had a warm relationship with Israel. He told me if I had money, I could study anywhere in the world. That put me at ease since I had $700 in my pocket. Little did I know that it was hardly enough for even the first year.

After a few hours, the plane landed in Tel Aviv, Israel. As soon as I got off, I could feel the warm and soft afternoon Mediterranean breeze. A uniformed airline employee was waiting to take me to my Air France flight. He treated me with respect and we chatted about the weather while walking to the terminal. About five or six hours later, we landed at Orly Airport in Paris. The airline put me in a nice hotel at the airport. I remember writing a long letter to my parents letting them know how much I loved them, appreciated their sacrifice, and promised to work and study hard to be successful, help society, and make them proud. Most of the time my eyes were full of tears. I was leaving behind my family and friends who appreciated my sense of humor, and I knew I was going to miss my mom's delicious cooking for a long time.

One of the highlights of my trip was stopping in London for a day to visit with my Aunt Noushi, who managed to get permission from her nun supervisor at the hospital to see me for a few hours. We met at Trafalgar Square. The beautiful historical statues and buildings, the water fountain, and countless pigeons were just amazing. The place made such an impression on me that, more than a decade later in the 1970s when I was the managing director of Admen Advertising Agency in Tehran,

we filmed a few commercials there for launching Bristol Myers Mum deodorants in Iran. I was amazed how London looked so much cleaner and more orderly than Tehran. I was also surprised by automatic doors, which I had to test several times to believe my eyes. It was a bit scary as the taxi was driving on the left side of the road to Heathrow, which was then called London Airport.

CHAPTER 2

Experiencing America's 1960s Counterculture

It was dark when our plane approached Washington National Airport in February 1964; the view of the city from the sky was dazzling. I had been dreaming of that moment for a long time and was ecstatic that I was finally in the United States. It was a long journey with stops in Tel Aviv, Paris, London, and New York. I was disappointed that my cousins were not at the airport to pick me up as my arrival date was lost in translation between Iranian and Gregorian calendars. I got into a cab and the driver picked up another passenger who seemed to be a businessman with a suit and tie who figured that I was new to the United States and told me the names of each iconic building on our way. Shortly before he got out at a hotel, he pointed to the Washington Monument, but I heard him say "Washington Money Man," which sounded right to me since I had seen the picture of Washington on my dollar bills. That was the first of many misunderstandings in America.

The driver dropped me off at the Woodner Hotel Apartments on 16th Street NW where my cousins Cyrus and Cameran lived. We were all excited to see each other. By then, Cyrus was about 23, had been in the US for three years, and was married to Linda to whom he showed quite a bit of romantic affection—quite unusual in Iran. I was not used to seeing that much hugging, back rubbing, handholding and cuddling in a family setting. They had a one-bedroom apartment with a TV and a hideaway sofa bed in the living room. The flooring was a very nice hard wood where Cameran put his mattress for me and slept on the box in the bedroom. Linda and Cyrus were sleeping on the sofa bed. We all went to bed after a long talk about how my uncle was doing and what I was planning to do.

Bejee, my uncle's ex-wife, had capitalized on her flair for fashion and had a boutique on Connecticut Avenue across from the Sheraton hotel. She had a house close to her business and was doing well. She had managed to get green cards for both of my cousins; Cyrus was working at Hecht Company, a large department store in downtown DC. Cameran had attended a computer class and was making a decent income working at an insurance company. Cyrus had just become the proud owner of a 1964 yellow Chevrolet Impala convertible, and Cameran had a black 1957 Chevrolet. Both brothers, who were brought up by my military uncle, were talented and disciplined. Linda worked at the Pentagon.

After staying a few days with my cousins, I found my friend, Mostafa, who was now Moe. People started calling me Fred, a shorter version of Fereydun. It was good that no longer I had to explain where my exotic name came from. Moe and I rented a one-room efficiency in a row house on Calvert Street, NW, in Washington DC. It was close to the Calvert Street Bridge over Rock Creek Park, renamed Duke Ellington Memorial Bridge in 1974. From our place, we could walk to Bejee's Boutique on Connecticut Ave.

There were two large hotels nearby, the Sheraton, across from Bejee's, and the Shoreham Hotel on the other side of the bridge on Calvert Street. Our row of houses was old but charming; although they all looked the same, they had different ornaments on their roofs. They constantly played "My Boy Lollipop" by Millie Small on the radio, I especially liked the part, "Love you I, Love you I." From an electrical store nearby, we rented a black-and-white TV with a rabbit ears antenna and a connected remote for a few dollars a week. Whenever I watched TV, I was reminded that I still had a long way to go in understanding everything. I spent quite a bit of time reading newspapers and listening to the radio while looking up words that were unfamiliar.

Politically, there was a lot going on: the Civil Rights Act of 1964 and the presidential elections. I listened to Senator Goldwater's speech explaining why he was voting against the Civil Rights bill; he was passionately arguing in the US Senate that the public accommodation and fair employment section of the bill was unconstitutional. It was hard to imagine that the United States of America, the beacon of democracy in the twentieth century, not giving every one of its citizens equal rights. Goldwater became the Republican Party candidate for president and eventually lost to Lyndon B. Johnson. Johnson was president the entire time that I was in the country as a student during the 1960s.

A one-legged man in front of a laundromat on Calvert Street sold evening papers by throwing them, one after the other, into cars and a young boy collected the money. A corner drug store nearby had a fast food and coffee counter; I tried cheesecake for the first time and liked it a lot. I went there for a cup of coffee and cheesecake so often that I learned to order without an accent. There were a lot of old people there, including the servers. I started to learn how to make small talk with strangers; the first question people asked me was where I came from and most of the servers had no idea where Iran was. There was a vending machine in the laundromat where I was introduced to Dr. Pepper, which I loved. To improve my English, I attended a free class at the School of Americanization close to Calvert Street during the summer of 1964. The teacher was a charming older lady who spoke slowly and was kind to students. The teaching material was light and fun about American history and the mainstream culture of the time. It included singing some popular songs like "Easter Parade" by Judy Garland and Fred Astaire. We also learned square dancing in class. I thought it was an effective and entertaining introduction to American mainstream cultures and customs, although the counterculture revolution was gradually starting.

Moe and I both wanted to work on our English and save money until September when the school year would begin. My dad, who knew I needed more money, wrote me letters with a red pen telling me that I should find a job. Moe's brother was a doctor in Montreal, Canada, and sent him money from time to time. Early on, our building janitor, a poor old white lady with many age spots on her face mentioned that the Sheraton hotel was always hiring. Moe started working at the Sheraton from 7 a.m. to 4 p.m. The pay was good, but his job was hard. He carried dirty dishes from the dining room through a long corridor under the building to the kitchen and returned with clean dishes and glasses. He also cleaned tables and served water and coffee whenever he was free. He was exhausted when he came home; it was funny to see the most dapper and popular person in our high school carrying dirty dishes.

Bejee suggested that I work next door to her boutique in a French restaurant called Napoleon on Connecticut Ave.

She introduced me to Mr. and Mrs. Polites, the French owners, and they agreed to hire me. They fed us employees at around 5 p.m., before work began. The first time I ate there, I noticed that everyone was laughing at me. Mrs. Polites approached me and nicely asked if I liked frog legs. I was disgusted at first, since I thought I was having chicken, but afterward, I decided that I liked frog legs. The small cozy restaurant in an old two-story building had an extensive French menu. The bar and dining room were on the second floor, and my job was to send the orders downstairs to the kitchen via a dumbwaiter and pull it up when someone from the kitchen yelled that the orders were ready.

The Friday night I started, the restaurant was packed with guests from the Sheraton hotel where there was a political conference going on. The dining room was full of well-dressed men and women passionately discussing politics. I heard the names Goldwater, Johnson, and Robert Kennedy float by. There were two men in black suits playing French romantic songs with violins.

I noticed that a large mouse was slowly going upstairs toward the dining room. I could not even imagine the pandemonium that the sighting of the mouse would have created, especially if it was noticed by one of those elegant ladies. The music and conversations were quite loud but fortunately, Mr. Polites was a heavyset man and saw it too. With one of his heavy medical shoes, he managed to strike the poor mouse dead and probably save his business.

I was beginning to understand the gist of guests' conversations and was surprised at how informed the women were, contrary to my perception of women in Iran who didn't seem to be interested in politics at the time. Occasionally, I went to the pantry in the restaurant to look up a word. Sometimes, customers asked me where I was from and their reaction was positive when I mentioned Iran; most of them associated it with the shah and Persian cats. I was unduly defensive about working in a restaurant since one's status was very important in Iran and working in a restaurant was quite low in the totem pole. People were quite encouraging when I proudly told them that I would be attending university in the fall. Most were quite friendly and wished me well.

My cousin, Cameran, told me that every Wednesday evening there was a dance at the YWCA, which was short for Young Women's Christian Association. We went there together and enjoyed punch that tasted like Kool-Aid. We saw many pretty young women standing on one side of the room. The guys would go and ask them if they would like to dance; most were accepting. I heard this was the place Cyrus had met Linda. I spotted a pretty blonde girl who was standing alone but it took several minutes for me to muster up my courage. As a slow romantic song started to play, I asked her if she would like to dance and she graciously accepted. After a little introduction, she put her cheek on mine; I was in heaven! She was a secretary working for the government. At that point, I had realized my expectations of all what I had imagined about America. After a while, the place was closing and she told me that she would see me next time, which I took it literally. Until the following Wednesday, I was naively thinking about our dance all the time and could not wait to see her again, thinking that she would be waiting for me too. The next Wednesday, we went a little later with high expectations, but to my great disappointment, I saw her dancing cheek-to-cheek with a tall, handsome sailor. I got a glimpse of the American go-getter culture and realized that I should have been there sooner.

On weekends, I often went with Cameran and Moe to Georgetown where there were lots of restaurants and bars with live bands, especially on M Street. We parked our car on a steep cobblestone street which they said was close to Jacqueline Kennedy's home. The place was very lively, full of young, friendly people going from one place to another. I remember a few names like Max, Round Table, The Cellar Door, and Silver Dollar. They normally charged $2.25 for a pitcher of beer, and a few had cover charges. One evening, we were in an elevator going to a dance with a group of Iranian friends. A tall, muscular man in the elevator was wearing a fedora with a feather on its side, a hat many American men were wearing in the early 1960s. The man had been drinking and his face was somewhat red. One of the boys who had just arrived from Iran, wanted to practice his English with the American. He pointed toward the man's hat and said "chicken." What he really wanted to ask was whether the feather came from a chicken, but it seemed like he was calling the guy a chicken. We could see the man was getting angry, but fortunately, the elevator door opened and we all jumped out.

Moe and I had been in the US for a few months and were missing our family and Iranian chelo kabob. We had tried an Arabic restaurant but the kabob was different and there was no basmati rice. We heard about a nearby place on the third floor of an old building called Iran House where they served chelo kabob for lunch on Sundays for only $1. When we went there on a Sunday, they were serving lunch to about 30 or 40 young people there in a large room. The food was exceptionally good, even better than some of the high-end restaurants in Tehran. After we had tea, the cook showed up and made a few remarks about the shah's widespread oppression of the Iranian people and he asked everyone to join the demonstration against the shah when he visited the United States that June.

We had no doubt this was part of the anti-shah student organization in the United States and the $1 chelo kabob was a gimmick to attract new Iranian students like Moe and me. Ironically, these students were benefiting from the new prosperity in Iran and the warm relationship between the two countries but were taking advantage of their newfound freedom in America by talking about creating a revolution in Iran.

The cook had been the personal chef of the Iranian ambassador to the US, Ardeshir Zahedi, whose father, General Zahedi, was the leader of the 1953 coup that ousted Mossadegh. Ardeshir was married to Princess Shahnaz Pahlavi, the shah's oldest daughter, and was famous for throwing lavish parties for American political and government elites at the Iranian embassy on Massachusetts Avenue in Washington DC. I heard the cook was not happy with what Zahedi paid him since he was highly talented and hardworking. So, he left the embassy and found a job at a major hotel in Washington DC for a lot more money. After the embassy threatened to arrest and deport him, he joined Iran House and helped them organize the Sunday luncheons for anti-shah outreach and recruitment. I believe Iran House was affiliated with the Confederation of Iranian Students that eventually contributed to the downfall of the shah.

I was still interested in becoming a commercial pilot and Cyrus thought military service might be the best way to achieve my goal. He asked one of his customers, a retired army colonel, to help me if he could. The colonel took me to an army recruiting office near the Hecht Company in downtown DC, but despite his enthusiastic efforts, they would not sign me up since I was not a permanent resident of the United States.

Finally, school was about to start so Moe went to UCLA and I stayed at a friend's apartment in Langley Park close to the University of Maryland for a few days before the dorms opened. My friend was constantly on the phone with his girlfriend discussing her pregnancy; she was determined to keep the child and my friend was wondering aloud how he might be able to break the news to his parents in Iran. He asked me for advice but I had no idea how he should handle his situation. Fortunately, after a week or so, it was time to move to the College Park campus as the fall '64 semester was formally beginning. I was so excited and looking forward to campus life.

When I entered my room on the fourth floor of Cambridge Hall, I met my Nigerian roommate. He suggested that we request to share rooms with American roommates so we could learn more about the culture and improve our English, including our accents. I thought it was a great idea and we asked our faculty resident, Mike, who made it happen. My new roommate was a nice person and a serious student although he occasionally smoked a pipe in the evenings. I couldn't stand the smell of his tobacco but was too shy to say anything to him.

I got a new roommate the following semester. He was a nice, soft-spoken guy who often mentioned that his dad had previously worked for the government in some undercover capacity but his coworkers had betrayed him. Cambridge Hall was the honors dorm, which made me wonder why I was there. Our building was an all-male dorm among four in that complex, two facing each other for men and two for women. The female dorms had house mothers who enforced curfew; female students could receive visitors before curfew which was extended during the weekends. The complex was within walking distance of Byrd Stadium and the student union, which had been built a decade earlier with upscale interior design and furniture. It also had a ballroom where they often had dance events with live bands. The dining rooms were in the middle and were open when classes were in session, except Sunday nights. They always had only fish for lunch on Fridays for religious reasons. In the dining halls, I frequently met students from all over Maryland. There were foreign students too, but most were from Iran, thanks to oil revenues and Iran's excellent relationship with the United States. Most of foreign students were studying math, physics, or engineering.

Drinking alcohol was prevalent among students. Some students decorated their walls with Playboy centerfolds and had empty bottles of hard liquor like vodka, gin, and whiskey around their room as souvenirs of their drinking events. The guys always bragged about drinking and having sex. Across from our room, was a guy who had left the Naval Academy in Annapolis, Maryland. He was quite tall and athletic but a big drinker and stayed in bed until late afternoon every day. Most students were in their rooms studying in the evenings.

During the first couple of months, I made a lot of friends. In those days, saying you were Persian was a good thing; quite a few people knew the shah. "Persian" sounded exotic and my accent helped too. Everyone had heard about Persian cats and some had come across the Persian Empire in their history books. Once a woman in the dining room told me that Persia was mentioned in the Bible, and Cyrus of Persia freed Jewish captives in Babylon. I was beginning to feel less of a total stranger. I was fascinated by campus life and the American lifestyle and was trying to participate in activities and assimilate as much as possible. I had managed to translate my sense of humor to the new environment and had fun with friends. Many dances were sponsored by various organizations on campus, mostly with live bands in the student union ballroom, armory or coliseum. They always played "Unchained Melody" and romantic songs like that.

Soon, it was time for the first home game of the University of Maryland Terrapins. I finally understood that the Terrapin bronze statue in front of the McKeldin Library was the football team's mascot. I heard things like "the Atlantic Coast Conference" and" Coach Tom Nugent," but was totally ignorant about the American football, not to mention my confusion as to why Americans called it *foot*ball, when the game was mostly played with the hands.

I went to see the first home game with some friends from the dorm. It was a nice fall day, and the yellow and red tree leaves on the walkway to Byrd Stadium were beautiful. Many students were walking to see the game with family and friends. It was all new to me and I discovered how big college football was. When we got inside the stadium, I was so impressed with how organized and orderly everything was; the uniforms were colorful and the cheerleaders were dazzling, not to mention the band and the halftime show. For the first time, I saw genuine American patriotism by how people respected the US flag. They stood up straight, put their hands on their hearts, and some sang the national anthem without anyone forcing them to do it.

Several weeks later I saw the Terrapins play Penn State Nittany Lions. They seemed like a very strong team and I noticed their very talented cheerleaders. In my wildest dreams, I could not imagine that I would be a professor of advertising at Penn State University two decades later, since neither teaching nor advertising were on my mind, not to mention Pennsylvania.

I signed up for aeronautical engineering as my major as it was the closest thing to aviation and satisfied my dad's wish for me to become an engineer. My introductory math class was easy and I got an A since we had quite a few math classes in high school in Iran. In the 1960s, high school students in Iran had three choices for their last three years: mathematics, natural sciences, or literature and women could also take home-making. I had taken the mathematics sequence, which included calculus, trigonometry, and geometry. One of my first classes in Maryland was engineering drawing, which I didn't like at all, but I enjoyed calculus and trigonometry. I found the whole engineering environment too boring and void of human relations and creativity.

I was beginning to have second thoughts about my major, especially since I learned that Iran Air, the flagship airline of Iran, was in financial trouble and there was no aeronautical industry in Iran in 1960s. That meant there would probably be no job for me when I went home even after all the money that my dad had spent. I was totally confused and anxious about my academic prospects and my financial situation considering the very high out-of-state tuition and other unanticipated expenses. I had no idea who to ask for advice. The foreign student advisor had little in the way of emotional intelligence and was of no help. He always looked distant when he was talking and repeated the same things. He had a friendly secretary who seemed to be a lot more helpful to students.

Soon, I had my first Thanksgiving dinner at the home of an English professor along with another Iranian student and two Nigerians who were wearing traditional outfits. At least two dinner items were totally new to me: stuffing and cranberry sauce. The professor told us about the history of the Thanksgiving, including the *Mayflower*, the pilgrims, and the first harvest celebration with the Native Americans.

After dinner others wanted to know more about our countries, cultures, upbringing, and so on. One of the ladies advised the Nigerian students to wear their Nigerian outfits in public whenever possible for their own security and safety, especially when traveling in the South. The other lady talked about anti-Semitic sentiments in the South.

Right after Thanksgiving, the spirit of Christmas was everywhere. We decorated our dorm and hung Christmas lights in the front of the building from the dorm windows. We constantly heard Christmas songs on the radio. I saw a group of female students from Centerville Hall holding candles and singing beautiful Christmas carols in front of Cambridge Hall. I was totally surprised how happy and encompassing Christmas celebration was at every level in America.

The university arranged for me and a Lebanese student to spend the Christmas holidays with a nice old lady who lived alone close to the border of Washington DC and Maryland in a charming old house. From her photographs, it was obvious that she had once lived there with her husband and children. She gave each of us our own room with a TV. I was starting to enjoy some sitcoms and shows although I didn't fully understand them.

On a Sunday morning, the lady took both of us to church and introduced us to her friends who were all wearing fancy fedora hats and welcomed us graciously. It was my first time in a church. While we were sitting on pews, I was wondering why people had to sit on the floor in the mosques. Later, she told me that people stood during church services in the old days. It was quite unexpected when everyone—people of all ages—started singing. The Lebanese student seemed to be more familiar with the church routine. We picked up a couple of books and went to the page that the lady showed us. After a couple of minutes into singing, I noticed everyone was looking at me and our hostess graciously pointed out my mistake: I was following the Farsi recitation of poetry, reading horizontally instead of moving down vertically from one verse to the next. My deep and loud voice accentuated the error of not being in sync with the others, not to mention my Farsi accent. Eventually, I got the hang of it, but the embarrassment stayed with me for a long time.

When we got home, the Lebanese student told me there was going to be a major war in the Middle East between Arab countries and Israel. He was on the side of the Arabs and was passionate about the Palestinian cause. He told me his grandmother could write and speak excellent English and his grandfather had been a lawyer who graduated from the American University of Beirut. He showed me a picture of his grandpa in the 1920s; he was very well dressed. When I asked him what the war was about, he told me that his ancestors, including his parents, had lived in Palestine peacefully for many years with their Jewish neighbors, but around 1948, everything changed and the Arabs were kicked out of their own homes.

He was hopeful that Egypt and other Arab countries would fight to get their homes back. I thought he was exaggerating, but low and behold, the war happened in June of the following year. In the Six-Day War, Israel managed to substantially expand its territory: the West Bank, including East Jerusalem from Jordan, Golan Heights from Syria, and Sinai and Gaza from Egypt. I guess for cultural, linguistic, geopolitical, and religious reasons the newly gained territories were neither integrated into the Israel proper nor could they be established as their own states. Unfortunately, generations of Palestinians and Israelis have been locked in conflict for decades.

By the end of my first year at the university, I had changed my major to economics with a minor in mathematics. It sounded a bit closer to what I liked compared to engineering. I felt so guilty that I had not lived up to my dad's expectations, both financially and academically. I was also worried about my brother Farrokh and what he could do after high school and I knew my dad was hoping that I could help him. But Farrokh made everyone proud and got accepted into the University of Tehran Medical School, the most prestigious in Iran. The entrance exam for the medical school was the hardest in the country; only 120 of twelve thousand participants were accepted. Later, my brother completed his residency in radiology at Loma Linda University and has been practicing in the United States for about 30 years.

During summer of 1965, my friend Ali and I moved off campus to an efficiency apartment on Biltmore Avenue in Washington, DC, very close to where Moe and I had lived a year before. I was quite familiar with the area but the apartment did not have air conditioning and was quite hot and humid at night. Unfortunately, Washington, DC was the only area where we could find odd jobs with decent wages. I got a job at the Washington Hilton working from early morning to late afternoon. I believe it was during that summer when Ali and I befriended a guy a couple of years younger than us, Miguel. He was from Cuba and was living a few houses down with a family. I believe a man in that household worked at the Shoreham Hotel nearby. We went to some outdoor concerts, and whenever we were crossing a bridge, Miguel walked on the edge and challenged us to follow suit; he was a brave and playful young man.

*****

Fast forward to an evening in 2021 in my home in Anaheim Hills, California. The TV was on in the background and in a fleeting moment, I saw a picture of what looked like a young Miguel on the screen. The show was a documentary about the life of Amazon's Jeff Bezos and his stepfather, Miguel, who raised him. I immediately googled to see if he was in Washington DC when I was. Low and behold, he had been there. It was so exciting to learn that the father of the richest man in the world could be our old friend, albeit for a short summer. Who knew then what life had in store for him?

*****

Back on Biltmore Street in 1965, I found a better job at Blackie's House of Beef on 22nd and M Street in DC, an iconic restaurant that Washington elites frequented. The restaurant was quite busy that summer. I had met the Augers who were the owners but did not know Lulu Auger was the founder. I heard they closed the place after Lulu's death around 2012. A Greek manager ran the dining rooms like we were in a combat zone. After a while, he gave me five tables. It was an intimidating place, and I was always afraid of losing my job. The kitchen was a chaotic place, and the chef was a central American gentleman who was quite sensitive and angry at all times; he abused his power in that kitchen. We tried hard not to get on his bad side. There was no room for error and if there was a complaint, the manager quickly determined that it was the server's fault. The tips were good, but the job was quite hectic and stressful.

The place was most popular and exceptionally busy on Friday and Saturday evenings. A huge guy with a cowboy hat stood in front of the restaurant and whistled for taxicabs. I worked there for most of the summer and had almost enough money to pay for tuition, room, and board.

When school started at the University of Maryland, they put me on the first floor of Easton Hall in a complex similar to the previous one. Denton Hall was one of the halls in that complex. Across from our complex on the other side of the University Boulevard, a large pond froze during winter and students ice skated on it. I tried it once and fell so many times that my body ached for days. My new roommate was a tall, lazy guy who mumbled and never completed his sentences. He was bored most of the time and looked everywhere for food late at night. There were no foreign students on our floor but most of the guys there were super nice, including our faculty resident, who was a wrestler,

One afternoon, early in the semester, 25 or 30 of us went to a bar nearby under the guidance of our faculty resident. Each of us ordered a pitcher of beer and took a turn drinking the entire thing without putting the pitcher down. Everyone chanted "chug-a-lug, chug-a-lug!" I was beginning to understand the game and was nervous because I did not want to be the loser, although I already had a good background in beer drinking. When it was my turn, I lifted the pitcher and started drinking to chants of "Here's Persian Fred, blue and true, chug-a-lug, chug-a-lug!" I took a breath a few times while keeping the pitcher close to my mouth. Everybody was clapping when I drank the last drop of beer. I felt so proud. Soon, our faculty resident told us to get out—the police were coming. The drinking age in DC was 18 but in Maryland it was 21; I think most of us were underage. This was my first introduction to states' rights. We soon scattered on a large grassy area, heading toward our dorms.

Most evenings after about 9 p.m. when we were done with our assignments, we got together in one of the dorm rooms and played no-limit Texas hold'em poker for pennies. A campus police officer, who oversaw our area, came to play with us until late at night. He was a heavyset old man who had a great sense of humor; when the dispatcher radioed to ask about his location, he'd clear his throat and report in a serious tone that he was in the dining room or the library.

On Friday nights when many students went home for the weekend, a designated student on our floor collected money and left the dorm with his luggage like the others. But he quickly returned with his luggage full of alcoholic beverages purchased from a liquor store on Route 1, across from the campus, for the weekend parties. Girls were prohibited from entering the men's dormitories, but once in a while, a few women came for a party.

I was enjoying my classes and learned quite a bit from my national economic planning course regarding private and public expenditures and investment. I took German for a couple of years, which helped me later when I was back in Iran and had German clients. I was doing okay at school, but a source of constant anxiety was my rapidly depleting finances.

My dad heard that I needed a car, so without asking me, he sent money he had bought on the black market to a friend who was visiting the US. The friend called me and showed up the next morning in front of the student union building. When he arrived, he started kissing me on both cheeks—a common Iranian greeting gesture—but I was embarrassed because there were many students around and tried politely to fend him off. Then he linked his little finger with mine as I was trying to walk away from the area; it was a sign of friendship among the older generation of Iranians, but not common in America. He meant well, but it did not fit the culture at the time. After all the pleasantries, he gave me about $500 and I bought my first car, a 1962 light blue Chevy II.

The next summer, a friend and I rented a double bunk room in a fraternity house. The house was empty and had no air conditioning, but it had a large kitchen and refrigerator that we could use. The house was on a fraternity row and we had to pass by one that had a sign in front of it "Negros and Jews

Need Not Apply." The sign still disgusts me when I think about it.

Having a car certainly expanded my employment options. I worked as a cashier in a valet parking garage where the Cuban manager was obsessed with security and constantly showed me different scenarios of how the employee drivers—all non-whites—might try to steal the cash. Soon, I found another cashier job at the National Airport in Washington DC where there was always an unending line of cars; I had to punch their tickets, manually compute their parking fees, and enter the number into the cash register. The pay was good but the manager had me sign my paycheck over to him and paid me in cash after deducting computational errors that I supposedly had made. I think he put the difference in his pocket. The pay was still good and was worth the long commute.

The car expanded my social life too. That summer, I spent a week in Ocean City, Maryland which reminded me of the Caspian Sea. We saw a show where the horse jumped off a platform and plunged into a pool below. I heard they discontinued that show because of animal protection laws. I tried my first ever roller coaster ride at Glen Echo Park in Virginia; we were so excited to sit on the front row and scream with everyone else. The ride was rather scary as the old structure was shaking so badly that sometimes we felt we were going to fall sideways.

As I settled down in America, things were definitely changing. My favorite songs, Millie Small's "My Boy Lollipop" that had been playing frequently on the radio when I first arrived in the US, and the Supremes' "Stop in the Name of Love," were overshadowed by the songs of the Monkees, the Beatles, the Beach Boys, and the Rolling Stones that I also loved. At parties,

I frequently heard Ravi Shankar, Bob Dylan, Joan Baez, and Judy Collins.

A bar-restaurant at the edge of the campus on Route 1, the Varsity Grill, had a large basement room with a dance stage and a platform on each side. Every evening, two young attractive women, the "go- go girls," danced on the platforms to popular songs like, "Somebody to Love" from Jefferson Airplane, "Wouldn't It Be Nice" by the Beach Boys, "Light My Fire" by Jim Morrison of the Doors, and "(I Can't Get No) Satisfaction" by the Rolling Stones. The *Summer Place* movie that attracted me to America seemed so innocent and distant; perhaps the *Easy Rider* movie depicting rebellion against established values around race, sex, alcohol, and drugs was more telling of the times.

The fast-food scene was changing too. Right across from the Varsity Grill was the hamburger joint White Castle. Apparently, it was a chain restaurant where relatively old men wore white uniforms and garrison hats and fried small, square burgers. They also had a jukebox where I heard the song "I'm a Believer" for the first time. Few students were there, indicating the joint was living on borrowed time. There were a couple of nice sandwich shops across Route 1 and I became fond of ham and cheese, which we did not have back home. A McDonald's was a short driving distance down Route 1; it was in a temporary building, if not a tent. I loved their double cheeseburgers and vanilla shakes. In those days, the only places where you could sit and talk were bars.

In 1967, I rented a two-bedroom apartment in a building on Knox Road, College Park, with three other students. My roommate, six-foot six-inches tall and quite heavy, was in love with steam locomotives and constantly played the ukulele and sang old steam locomotive songs in a coarse voice. In the other room were two smart Jewish guys, cousins or close friends from New York. One was a hippie-type guy with longer hair; the other, a little bit older, had a shorter haircut and wore regular clothes. They both held strong anti-war and anti-establishment attitudes, which was common among students on campus at that time. We became friends and had many intellectual discussions.

The building, owned by Professor Perkins, had two bedrooms, a living room, kitchen, bath, and a refrigerator. You could smell weed in the apartment most of the time. My roommates passed around a homemade bong but refused to give it to the ukulele guy whom they thought was unstable, and for good reason. I once returned home to pandemonium in front of our building. There was a crowd around the ukulele roommate who had gotten hold of some marijuana and was quite high. He was crying loudly and out of control. He finally managed to calm down and went to bed, snoring most of the night. So many drinking and smoking parties were under the guise of anti-establishment and anti-war movements. My roommates had late-night parties where everyone smoked marijuana. One night when I went to see what was going on, a friend was body painting some female students who lived nearby.

I don't remember seeing a Black student during that time. Unfortunately, there was much racism in 1960s America, in spite of lessons learned from the past: Rosa Park refusing to give her bus seat in Montgomery, Alabama, more than a decade earlier, Martin Luther King, Junior's iconic dream speech eight years later, not to mention the passage of the Civil Rights Act in 1964. One summer in the late 1960s, I was working at a restaurant in Arlington, Virginia that belonged to Tom Sarris' ex-wife. An older man and his two sons were having dinner when a Black family entered the restaurant and was seated somewhere out of the way where they were not very visible. The older man dining with his sons got up, threw his napkin on the floor, and angrily— and loudly—said that he wouldn't eat where a [the N word] family eats. I felt so sorry to see the facial expressions of the Black family's children. Nobody was shocked when the old man and his sons left the restaurant without finishing their food. Black people were totally segregated; you seldom saw a Black student at university, a Black bank teller, or even a Black server in a restaurant—unless you went into the kitchen. An Afghan student always talked about the plight of Black people and was very much involved in the Black Muslim movement in New York.

To save money, I moved into a large, narrow room in the basement of a five-story building on Knox Road, next to the building where my old roommate was frequently playing ukulele and singing steam locomotive songs. The rent was cheap and I shared the room with two other people, Lou and Steve. I'm sure the room did not comply with the city rental code since it had only a small window and most of the room didn't get sunlight. Another room across a small hallway next to a utility room without a window was rented to a Vietnamese student. He told me that in Vietnam, like in Iran, they played their national anthem in movie theaters before the film started and everyone was forced to stand up in respect if they didn't want to get arrested. The landlord fixed everything himself, including toilets in the middle of the night. It turned out we were the last tenants in that basement.

71

Steve was a PhD student from New York who constantly analyzed me and Lou. On the floor above us, four female students shared an apartment; one was Christie, a popular girl on campus. She used to come downstairs to get cookies from Lou, who always had some in his desk drawer. One night, she found naked pictures of men in Lou's desk drawer, including a naked man with a sailor hat and another lifting weights. The news of the pictures traveled fast and everyone was shocked. Lou was gay and didn't deny it, but the landlord was quite angry and asked Lou to leave the property immediately. When I asked the landlord why Lou had to leave so quickly, he told me he wanted to protect the reputation of his building since students wouldn't rent from him if the word got out that he was renting to Blacks and gays. The landlord was a Polish immigrant who seemed to be anti-Semite, racist, and anti-gay. He complained that he had seen girls making out with each other when fixing things in their apartments, but unlike Lou, they had a rental contract and the landlord couldn't do anything about it.

I was constantly looking for jobs that would pay enough for my out-of-state tuition and other expenses. A few friends wanted to work as a taxi driver during summer since the hours were flexible and the pay was good so we all started working at the Yellow Cab Company. On our first day, one of our friends got a bit confused and backed onto a pile of construction material right inside the garage. His open microphone broadcast to our cab radios the sound of his engine as he frantically stepped on the gas pedal to no avail. The poor guy was fired on the spot. We still get a laugh during our reunions in Vegas when we talk about that day with our friends. One of those drivers became a gastroenterologist, and another became an electrical engineer and a successful investor.

The cabs were large, late-model American cars equipped with an automatic transmission and a radio to hear the dispatcher announce pick-up locations. He knew the area like the back of his hand. On a manifest, we recorded pickups, destinations, and fares. We put 60 percent of the cash in an envelope and dropped it in a box after we were done. Surprisingly, the driving job was quite interesting; I met and talked with all kinds of people. I picked up many Vietnam War soldiers who were released from the Walter Reed Army Hospital on Georgia Avenue, Washington, DC, close to our taxi offices. Most were dispassionate about the war and of those who talked, it was usually about their injuries, fallen friends, malaria, and other misfortunes of the war. They were mostly my age and friendly. I befriended a couple of them and occasionally had beer when I was off. Their war stories were horrible and they were all traumatized by what they had seen or done.

One soldier told me that he flunked out of the university, was drafted, and sent to Vietnam where he had to stand in a rice paddy with water up to his waist, holding a gun and watching for what he called "Charlies," the Viet Cong. He said they could attack from anywhere, including treetops. The sad thing was that the war was still raging and reporting large casualties on both sides in the media every day. Whenever I was around the Walter Reed, it was gut-wrenching to see young people my age with missing limbs or partially paralyzed in wheelchairs.

The justification for the war was that if South Vietnam became communist, there would be a "domino effect" spreading communism to all Southeast Asia. I heard a candidate for the US Senate promising "the Vietnamization of the war." He suggested letting the South Vietnamese do the fighting instead of Americans. Looking at the plight of those young soldiers, none of the arguments made sense to me.

Passengers had other stories. I picked up a middle-aged man from Holy Cross Hospital in Silver Spring, Maryland. As an accident victim who had just been released, he was furious that his wife didn't go see him at the hospital. We had a long conversation, and when he got out he told me to make sure that if I had a nice house like his when I got to his age, I should have someone waiting there for me. One early evening, an intoxicated passenger who was an Arab-American restaurant owner was so angry and offended that a hotel in Silver Springs, Maryland hadn't cashed his check. He accused them of racism and insisted I should go to his restaurant all the way in DC to see how rich he was. His restaurant happened to be in a scary neighborhood and he invited me inside where he gave me the fare and a big tip. One late night, shortly after I picked an attractive female passenger from a restaurant, she told me that she was trying to escape her older, abusive boyfriend who was following us and had a gun. I was so worried that he might shoot us but had no choice but to drive. That was the scariest moment of my entire time in the United States. I quickly got on I-495 freeway and took the next exit to some side streets and thank God, managed to lose him. After driving long hours during the summer and Christmas holidays, not to mention having a couple of serious near misses, I felt the job was a bit too dangerous, decided it wasn't worth the risk, and quit.

By late 1968, I had completed my major in economics and minor in mathematics but I wasn't excited about it; I had a feeling that I was on the wrong track in life. I wasn't even sure about what I could do in economics with my undergraduate degree in the United States without a work permit. The constant news of North Vietnam bombings and campus protests deepened my anxiety and pessimism. I was tired of doing odd jobs and was always short of money. I needed to complete my general education courses, but under no condition was I going to ask my elderly father for additional money; he had already sacrificed quite a bit for me. Without being registered full-time, my student visa would expire in a few months. I sadly knew if I left, I wouldn't be able to return to the US any time soon as I would be drafted into the Iranian Imperial Armed Forces and serve two years in a remote location in Iran. Despite the fact that I still needed quite a bit of money to complete a degree that I didn't like, the most painful thought was how disappointed my dad would be when I returned home without a university degree and the certain embarrassment in front of friends and family.

I had drifted far from my original values and goals; I felt neither Iranian nor an American at that time. I was struggling to understand myself, my identity, and what would make me happy. I felt like my life was over. I was constantly searching for options without finding one that appealed to me. I longed for advice and wanted to sit with and chat with my dad about everything under the sun over a cup of tea, like in the old days, before it was too late. I needed his guidance. I decided to go home and face all the risks and embarrassment that it entailed. It was a counterintuitive decision but turned out to be one of my best.

CHAPTER 3

Discovering My Hidden Strengths in a Prosperous Iran

On a gloomy evening in February 1969, I arrived at JFK Airport to catch my flight to Luxembourg for the first leg of my long journey back to Iran. During the five years I had lived in America, I witnessed a tumultuous time marked by the civil rights movements, the counterculture revolution, and frequent protests against the Vietnam War. As the large turboprop aircraft prepared for takeoff, I felt sad about leaving behind friends and my favorite places and that I would not be able to return to the US for a long time. I was wondering how my family, especially my dad, would react to me returning without a US university degree. Nonetheless, I was excited to see my dad and mom, my little sister, Fariba, who was only nine years old when I left, and my brothers Farrokh and Farhad who were attending college in Iran. I knew I would soon be drafted into the Iranian Imperial Army and had no idea what it was going to be like.

The cabin was packed with American young people with long hair, beaded necklaces, and colorful clothing. The flight attendants were generous in serving complimentary wine despite Icelandic Airlines having the lowest fare to Europe. The wine certainly helped allay the anxiety of aircraft noise and the bumpy ride. There was much energy on the air; I heard a guitar and singing mixed with loud conversations. The guy sitting next to me had a long beard and was wearing suede boots and a psychedelic shirt. He told me that he lived in Greenwich Village in New York and was heading to India. He reminded me of my roommate who used to smoke weed out of a homemade bong and occasionally arranged body-painting parties in our apartment. People compared notes on foreign currency exchange rates, hostels, and railroad schedules. In the middle of the night, we had to change planes in Reykjavik, Iceland's capital and largest city. We all walked to the new plane in the freezing cold; when we were airborne, the lights went out and the cabin was very quiet.

We landed in Luxembourg the next day in the late afternoon. The place was so peaceful and everything seemed much slower than in the US. The lady collecting money for bus tickets going to town was quite relaxed, taking her time, smiling, greeting, and chatting with everyone. She acted like she had all the time in the world. I stayed at a hostel with the American friend from the flight. The next day, I took a train to Munich about 370 miles away. I was surprised by how much more advanced the rail system was in Europe than the United States. I spent a night in Munich, the Bavarian capital, and the next morning, took a train to Istanbul. This was going to cover about 1,200 miles—through Germany, Austria, old Yugoslavia, Bulgaria, and Turkey. There was only one other person in our compartment.

I looked at the scenery outside and read a magazine. I enjoyed the pleasant ride through Germany and Austria, the food in the restaurant was much better than I expected, and the service was excellent. As we arrived at the border of old Yugoslavia, two border guards came to our compartment, rough and rude. One of them grabbed my *Playboy* magazine and told me it was not allowed there. That was my first encounter with a communist regime. When walking in the corridor to go to the restaurant car a short while later, I saw several guards in a compartment with their eyes absolutely riveted on the magazine's centerfold. I thought what liars and hypocrites they were. As the train moved eastward, the passengers looked poorer and the quality of food and services gradually dropped.

The constant clickety-clack sound of the train rolling was driving me crazy. I also was getting a bad cold. The guy in my compartment introduced himself as an engineer. He spoke some English and told me he was a displaced Palestinian living in Jordan. We had a long talk about the Middle East, Iran, and other issues. I did not fully agree with him on everything, but he seemed like a nice man. He was planning to get off in Sofia, the capital of Bulgaria, and stay there for a few days to buy a car. I did not know much about Bulgaria except for the nice Bulgarian feta cheese that my mom would buy for breakfast and the country's strong wrestling team that occasionally visited Tehran.

I really needed a break from the train and decided to stop in Sofia for a few days, especially since everything there was so inexpensive. I stayed in the same hotel as my Jordanian friend. Sofia seemed many years behind time; there were no signs of 1960s music or lively places like Macs and Round Table I had visited in the Georgetown area of Washington DC. I was told that Balkan Tourist was the happening place in Sofia. There was a restaurant on the top floor of the hotel where time had frozen in the 1940s and early 1950s. Bulgarian communist elites and some foreigners were dancing to the sound of a live band playing Frank Sinatra and Glen Miller. The beer tasted awful.

The next morning, I went for a walk around Sofia, home to magnificent old cathedrals and other historical buildings like what you find in many European cities. The streets were mostly cobblestone and clean. People looked poor but had clean clothing; I did not see any beggars. I took a bus to go to another part of town but did not know that I should have bought a ticket in advance. When the conductor asked for my ticket, a few passengers offered me theirs; it was such a nice gesture. I tried to give money to the guy who gave me his ticket but he refused to take it. Later, I went to a bank where many employees were working with big calculators at desks in a large area behind the counter. After examining the traveler's check I wanted to cash and going back and forth with another employee several times, they informed me that the nearest place to cash that check was in Athens, Greece, about five hundred miles away. I was shocked and it suddenly dawned on me how much I already missed the convenience of living in United States. I decided to take the train to Athens.

I was excited to visit a country with a long history of fighting ancient Persian armies with sensational victories and defeats. I was also looking forward to having my favorite Greek food, a real moussaka, and listen to some Greek music. But going to Athens from a communist country in 1969 was a lot more involved than I had imagined. The train was almost empty. I was reading *One-Dimensional Man*, a 1964 book by philosopher Herbert Marcuse whose ideas resonated with a lot of young anti-war groups and were popular among the critics of the so-called "military-industrial complex." The book was a critique of both capitalist and communist industrial societies. He argued that industrialized societies create false needs through advertising and mass media, which in turn leads people to see their worth and identity in the products they produce, own, or consume. Little did I know that I would spend 50 years of my life as a practitioner, professor, and researcher in the field of advertising and communication.

A young Belgian man shared my cabin, an aspiring journalist who was touring the world before he was going to settle down. When the train reached the border with Greece, it stopped for an exceptionally long time. After a while, I saw our train car was standing all alone in the middle of nowhere, waiting for the Greek side to pull it over. The Belgian offered me a beer and we had a nice long talk about every subject under the sun. I gave him my parents' address and told him that if he ever traveled to Tehran, he would be welcome to come and stay at our house. Frankly, I did not think that he ever would.

In Greece, I saw an unusual number of military personnel traveling on the train to Athens. Many were standing in the corridors and some were putting on their ties and straightening their military uniforms. It seemed they were responding to an emergency. Ironically, the oldest democracy was run by a group of dictatorial far-right military officers called the Greek Junta during that period.

In Athens, I visited the Acropolis, the most iconic monument of ancient Greece and the mythical home of gods and kings; it reminded me of Persepolis, the capital of Achaemenid Empire (550-330 BC) located outside of Shiraz, Iran. There were some structural similarities between the two as they both were built to project power, but I thought Persepolis was more magnificent. Surely, just bias on my part.

After a short visit, I returned to Sofia and picked up my luggage from the hotel and was rushing to catch a train when I saw the Jordanian in the lobby speaking to several people who seemed to be quite respectful. He spoke in Arabic mixed with a few German words; I think he was doing something more serious than merely buying a car in Sofia. I was a bit surprised to see quite a few Palestinian men in that hotel. I ran into an Iranian in the lobby who also used the title "engineer" before his name when he introduced himself. Many people in that part of the world and in Iran use engineer as a title, like "doctor." When I asked him about Iran, he mentioned that business was very good and there were many entertaining commercials on television.

After spending many hours on the train, I was finally in Istanbul—a magnificent city dividing Europe and Asia by means of the Bosporus Strait, a waterway about 20 miles long. In the evening, I went out for a beer and met a few Turkish university students who wanted to speak English with me and learn about America. They invited me to a bar where we met a Catholic priest who joined our table and we had a heated political discussion. It seemed there was much tension between the government and the opposition, especially the students and workers who were against Turkey's relations with the United States; they were objecting to the American Sixth Fleet visit to Istanbul happening around that time. There was much anti-American sentiment in Turkey.

Since both Turkish and Farsi were affected by years of Arabic influence through Islamic domination, they share quite a few common words and it's possible to communicate with people who knew very little English. In addition, the Turkish alphabet is Latin, which makes communication with the West somewhat easier. The changed alphabet was part of modernization and industrialization efforts initiated by Mustafa Kemal Ataturk, the founder of modern Turkey. Both Ataturk and Reza Shah, the founder of the Pahlavi dynasty in Iran, made great efforts to modernize and industrialize their countries in the face of much entrenched religious and cultural resistance. Ataturk created a republic in Turkey while Reza Shah continued a new monarchical regime in Iran.

In Istanbul, Turkey, I took a train to Erzurum, which is about eight hundred miles away from Istanbul and a few hundred miles from the Iranian border, Bazargan. The train reached Erzurum, a city in Eastern Anatolia, in the late afternoon. The city was about 210 miles from the Iranian border crossing of Bazargan, the most important ground border for importing and exporting goods. I immediately heard a man saying "Tabriz, Tabriz." I saw a bus from an Iranian company, Meehantour, was going to Tabriz, a Turkish speaking city located in the Northwestern part of Iran in the Azerbaijan province. As soon as I got onto the bus, I heard one of the classic songs of Marzieh, an Iranian popular female vocalist, on the bus record player. The song translation was "The Chinese Portrait Painter," which I had heard many times when I was growing up in Iran. I immediately felt at home. During the 360-mile trip to Tabriz, I noticed many rural and poor people. The level of service and cleanliness on the trains had declined consistently since we left the Austrian border. Hardly anyone spoke English, and when they did, their first question was why Iran was buying so many arms from the US. What for?

I was the sole translator for many hippie-type young European and American men and women on the bus. When the bus arrived at the Bazargan border, we ate at a restaurant that served Persian cuisine, including chelo kabab popular in Iran; some consider it a national food. It is marinated beef threaded on skewers grilled directly on fire served with saffron basmati rice, grilled tomato, butter, and a few other things. It was so good to taste a genuine chelo kabab after so many years. We also had dough, a customary drink in Iran, which is a mix of carbonated water and yogurt and a drink that most Americans don't like at all.

We arrived in Tabriz around early evening. After checking into a hotel, the Europeans asked me if I could go out on the town with them. I accepted, but after a short walk, I realized the nightlife in Tabriz was dead. People from that city, like most people in Azerbaijan, are ethnic Turks; they speak a version of the Turkish language and are serious, frugal, and highly religious people. The next day, I took a shower, shaved, put on some fresh clothes to make a dignified arrival home, and took an Iran Air flight to Tehran. The plane was almost full but most passengers were nicely dressed and polite. An hour later, we landed in Mehrabad International Airport, from where I had left for the US five years earlier with much hope and aspiration. I was so excited to see my family and friends that nothing else mattered at that moment.

As the taxicab drove through the city, I saw quite a few tall buildings and modern shops. Tehran had been dramatically modernized since I had left. Everything had been built up and you could hardly see any vacant land. The traffic was terrible but we finally reached my parents' house that was off Roosevelt Avenue in the Abbas Abad area. Every address was a mini direction in Iran. It was a three-story home with three complete apartments with bathrooms and kitchens. My parents used to rent out the third floor for additional income.

Finally, I was at the door of our old house with a pounding heart. When I rang the bell, Fariba, my lovely little sister, opened the door. She was now a beautiful, tall 14-year-old girl.

I was so happy to see her and could not believe how much she had grown in five years. It was the same with my brothers Farhad and Farrokh. Everyone was much taller than when I left. I felt guilty for not having stayed in closer touch with each of them. Farhad was completing his last undergraduate year at the School of Mass Communication, and Farrokh was completing his last years at the prestigious University of Tehran Medical School. My dad was about 73 and looked much older than when I had left, but my mom was cheerful and kind just as before.

Astonishingly, about a week later, the Belgian journalist who I had met on the train from Sofia to Athens showed up at our door. After spending a day with him, I took him to spend a day with my maternal uncle, Mohsen, a university professor who spoke fluent French, one of the official languages of Belgium. Mohsen was living with my grandparents, Hashem and Farah. When my Belgian friend came back that evening, he seemed very happy. He said he had so much fun that day and that it would be one of the most memorable highlights of his trip. I was surprised that instead of talking about his conversations with my uncle, he was mostly talking about my grandpa, Hashem, who told him lots of funny stories in Farsi that were translated by my uncle into French.

When the Belgian went back home, he sent me a nice letter thanking me for our hospitality and mentioned that he was going to marry soon. He also sent several large pictures of himself and my grandpa smoking opium. I was totally shocked; the pictures could get my grandpa arrested for sharing his medicinal opium with a European visitor. Opium was strictly banned for those who did not have doctor's permit and special coupons, and smugglers were sentenced to death. The Belgian had used Grandpa Hashem's vintage pipe that consisted of a stem and a detachable ceramic bowl on which there was an elegant picture of a Qajar king from the previous Iranian dynasty. It seems that in the old days, the pipe bowl was used as a mass medium to register the king's image at an opportune moment when the receiver was high. I got rid of the pictures but now I wish I had kept them.

Soon it was time for the Nowruz celebration. When I was growing up, it was my mom's favorite holiday; she always had the house painted or touched up and had pansies planted in our backyard. She made sure we all wore our new suits, shirts, and shoes before sitting around the traditional Haft Seen table. There were seven symbolic items on the table, whose names started with "seen," the 15th letter of the Farsi alphabet. Each item had meaning that had been carried forward from many centuries. We had sabzi polo and Caspian white fish for dinner, a traditional meal for Nowruz. That was the only time we saw our dad kiss our mom on her cheek.

When we were growing up, my mom used to take us to visit our great grandpa whom everyone called Haj Agha, and his wife. My mother's extended family was quite large, and most of them had moved from Mashhad to Tehran. There were countless people in the house, including many children. Everyone was in new clothing and was there to pay respects to the oldest members of the family and celebrate Iranian New Year. Haj Agha gave everyone a brand-new one-rial coin as a Nowruz present for good luck. We visited most of our extended family, starting with the oldest members and they paid a return visit during the two-week Nowruz holidays. We children received crisp new bills as gifts at every house we visited for Nowruz greetings; some family members were more generous than others. Our second stop for the Nowruz visit was my mom's parents. Our mom particularly loved her father, Hashem, whom we called Agha Joon, meaning dear sir. He instilled in her a great sense of humor and love for classic Farsi poetry. Sadly, when I returned in 1969, Haj Agha and his wife had already passed and my grandparents were quite old. Nowruz didn't seem to have its old flavor and most people were not following the Nowruz tradition. By and large, people were traveling and Tehran looked empty during the Nowruz holidays. That year, we took a trip with my aunt's family to spend about a week in Esfahan. I had been there before, but now I was truly appreciating its magnificent historic heritage.

The entertainment scene had revolutionized since my visit there about a decade earlier. Many restaurants were serving alcohol and quite a few had live music and dancing. One evening, we were at one of those restaurants where some young people were dancing to Iranian pop music. I asked a young friendly looking woman at the next table for a dance but as she was getting up, a few men—probably her brothers or cousins—surrounded me. They all calmed down when she invited me to sit at their table, but everyone was carefully listening to our conversation with much curiosity. Esfahan was a conservative city, and what I thought was a normal thing was quite offensive to the family. She told me she studied in Canada but wasn't like other girls and quickly turned the conversation to the subject of marriage. She asked me why I hadn't married in America, a conversation I wasn't ready to continue.

When we got back from Esfahan, I went to the National University of Iran to see the head of the economics department, Dr. Bahaman Amini. I had my transcript from the University of Maryland together with a letter from Professor Dudley Dillard indicating that I had completed the university requirements for a major in economics and a minor in mathematics. Dr. Amini seemed to have a strong affinity for Dillard since he got somewhat emotional when he saw his name in the bottom of the letter. I think it was great for National University to accept most of my credits from the US, but I still needed to take about a year and a half of coursework to graduate. The sweetest thing was that as long as I was studying there, I no longer needed to do my military service. Next, I had to find a job. I was constantly searching, but to no avail. Most employers required evidence of military service completion and a university bachelor's degree. Unfortunately, I had neither.

A friend told me that the Iranian Imperial Airforce was in dire need of English instructors and were not asking for a university degree nor were they interested in the status of my military service. The Imperial Airforce was the centerpiece of the shah's vision of making Iran the most powerful country in the Middle East. In doing so, he was buying large fleets of aircrafts from the United States and sending pilots and other personnel to the United States for specialized training in the operation and maintenance of the new equipment. I took a cab to the Air Force base southeast of Tehran. I passed their written and oral tests and attended a rigorous monthlong training, without pay, before I started teaching. Our students had four months of intensive English language instruction after boot camp before they could go to the US to receive their specialized technical training. The language curriculum was based on standard operating procedures published by the US government for use around the world.

My students were all going to be *Homafar*, a new category of non-commissioned officers designated for technicians. Most of them resented their lower status compared to commissioned officers. In fact, they were known for insubordination during the shah's reign and played a major role in the 1979 Islamic Revolution. They mainly came from provinces and working families. The instructors were mostly young Europeans and Americans who were kind and collegial; a lot of them were working temporarily to get some money and move on. The Air Force also provided transportation to and from our house, but the salary was rather low. I started to pay for my share of living with my parents. There was some socializing outside of the Air Force, and some colleagues were active in the Tehran Little Theater that I think was sponsored by the Iran-American Society. The Air Force job was temporary, and I continued looking for long-term professional employment opportunities without success.

As they say, sometimes the best things in life happen by accident. One day, my cousin Shahram and I were searching for movie showtimes in a newspaper when a job advertisement in classified section of the *Kayhan* newspaper caught my eye. The ad, in English, was looking for someone who spoke English and Farsi and could work without supervision in an advertising agency. I read it again and again—unlike other employment advertisements, there was no mention of either a university degree or military service. I loved the part about working without supervision. That afternoon, my life was changed forever.

I visited Caspian Advertising, Inc. where two Brits, Tony and John, interviewed me. They were sitting behind two connected clean, white face-to-face desks. John was a copywriter and Tony was an account person. The first question Tony asked me was whether I had any advertising experience; my response was no, but I qualified it by saying that I had seen many commercials in the US. John spoke Farsi well, both men were married to Iranian women and were hired by Ahmad Abdoli, the managing director of the agency and a medical doctor who was quite intelligent and diplomatic. Tony and John were primarily servicing the European and American companies. The Abdoli brothers—who also became medical doctors—were working in the accounting department. The fourth brother, Mark, was studying advertising in the United States. Tony and John invited me to lunch the next day and offered me a starting salary double what the Air Force was paying me. It was a happy moment and the beginning of a 50-year career in advertising and communication as a practitioner, researcher, and educator. That day, we had a few bottles of the Persian beer *Shams* and that was later became a client of mine. The Brits smoked a cheap Persian cigarette called *Zar*.

In the early 1970s, I felt a sense of optimism everywhere in Iran. The oil revenue was increasing, mass media was expanding, and consumer spending was growing rapidly. The shah was implementing his White Revolution creating a stable secular government as well as building a strong international image for Iran, capitalizing on his Western education, multilingual skills, and intimate familiarity with the Western culture. His promise of a great civilization seemed within reach; women were major beneficiaries of a secular government by participating in the workforce and being major decision-makers in household purchases. Iran was becoming the single largest consumer market outside of the US, Europe, and Japan, attracting international investments evidenced by countless joint-venture industrial entities in the country. The advertising industry was becoming a productive partner in modernizing the country by introducing many new products and services.

One of the shah's major public relations projects was the 2,500-year celebration of the Persian Empire that was founded by Cyrus the Great. The celebration promoted Cyrus as a national hero and featured the pre-Islamic origin of the country with a focus on the secular and monarchical tradition of Iran. Many world leaders participated in the dazzling festivities which also showcased the current artistic and modern achievement of the country under the shah. Critics were pointing to the high cost of the big splashy extravaganza and its focus on the international community as opposed to Iranians, not to mention the omission of Iran Islamic heritage. They argued that most Iranians were excluded from the celebrations, characterizing it as an exclusive royal party for elites and foreign dignitaries. It seemed that the event was more about the shah than the people of Iran. In my view, the significance of the celebrations as an investment and the promotion of the country was not properly and accurately communicated to the Iranian people by open discussions and commentary in the mass media, especially television.

Television coverage and TV set ownership rapidly rose in Iran, creating a fertile ground for advertising in an expanding economy as oil money poured in. Iranian national television had recently merged with the Radio Iran, forming the National Iranian Radio and Television (NIRT). Caspian, Inc. was under a $20 million contract with the NIRT to act as wholesaler for all television advertising in Iran. Abdoli had taken a risk and was being rewarded handsomely. I liked the fact that he trusted me and gave me the space and autonomy to grow while making money for the company.

My first client visit with Tony and John was to Starlight, an Iranian retail chain that distributed stockings and women's underwear products under the German brand Triumph. We discussed a commercial that had been produced by a young Iranian filmmaker, Ali who was educated in Germany and had a small studio called Cinegraphics where he and his German wife were living. Their apartment was a professional film studio during the day and, with some modification, was a warm home in the evening. Ali and I became good friends and made many commercials together. Ali became quite successful, and after the 1979 Islamic Revolution, he went to the United States and established IRTV in the Los Angeles area, which was the first Iranian television program in the US.

I started my advertising work with a small client, the International Wool Secretariat, and provided support for our international accounts. Correspondence with international clients was in English. It was interesting that the leadership of many Iranian companies was being replaced by the young Western-educated sons and daughters of the older entrepreneurs, and they preferred English correspondence for sharing information with their foreign partners and Farsi for domestic, media, vendors, and clients. The agency had a creative director, an art director with a team of artists, and account groups. Female account executives were handling Tide detergents and Camay soap by

Procter & Gamble, as well as the Bayer account. Several competitors, including Ziba Advertising Agency, had a relationship with McCann Ericson. Later, Englishman Richard Burlingham was put in charge of their international accounts.

After several months of working at Caspian, Inc., John and Tony left the agency to set up their own shop and part of their responsibilities were given to me. I was handling BF Goodrich, National Panasonic, Triumph International, Japan Airlines, and several other accounts. Caspian also hired a Swiss to work on accounts. In the meantime, I was dragging out graduation as long as I could to avoid the military service. I was immersed in the business of advertising, spending most of my time in client and creative meetings and presentations. I was discovering talents and capabilities that I never knew I had. I loved my job and was reading any American marketing and advertising book that I could lay my hands on.

Iranian women were becoming more assertive and confident. For example, when we conducted a phone survey about bras, almost all women responded and freely discussed their issues. The most important and frequent problem they mentioned was uncomfortable poking wires. The Triumph production group in Iran addressed the problem and we incorporated the notion of comfort in our advertising together with the European theme of glamour and sexuality in our national advertising with great success. I don't believe their mothers would have talked to a stranger, much less about their bra problems.

Around 1971, my client Japan Airlines invited me to an advertising meeting for Europe and Asia in London. I was eager to go and was planning to visit Triumph International in Munich, Germany but it seemed impossible for me to get a passport to travel abroad without having completed my military service. As a long shot, I called our old neighbor, General Shayanfar. He was working at the Imperial Inspectorate under his old friend, General Hossein Fardoust, the shah's childhood friend and one of the most powerful men in Iran. My brothers and I had grown up with his sons Farbod and Farivar. His wife accompanied me to the gendarmerie's headquarters in charge of compulsory enlistment for military service. There, we met with a captain who told me I must get a travel permission letter from the university and have it approved by the ministry of higher education before he could waive the military requirement. He also needed a bank certificate for several thousand dollars as a guarantee for my return.

It was a long road but certainly worth the effort. Caspian, Inc. arranged the certificate with no questions asked. I also got the other documents and went with the captain to get the document signed by his boss, a bald lieutenant general with an extremely large, elegantly framed picture of the shah behind him on the wall. After the captain performed a military salutation, he put the documents on the general's desk and the general quickly signed the letter without even looking at it. After he gave me the signed letter, the captain asked for my telephone number and called me that evening. He politely told me that he wanted me to buy him an army trench coat while in Germany so he could place his three stars on each shoulder. He told me that he would pay for it but I knew it was supposed to be a gift for his help.

Soon, I was back in Munich and was amazed by how much my life had changed since I was there two years earlier. I had been almost broke, and was heading into an absolutely uncertain life. This time, I was an advertising practitioner visiting my client, Triumph International. Iran was a large emerging market for many products, including Triumph's intimate apparel. The company's 1970s theme was women's beauty and sexuality. At their office in Munich, the Triumph International people showed me their new lines and mentioned a little bit about the modest beginning of the company and its founder Spiesshofer. They also gave me a nice tour of the beautiful Bavarian castles and gardens and occasionally showed me a mark of bullet or some signs of WWII. Later, I bought the trench coat for the captain with the help of a secretary and took a train to Frankfurt to catch a flight to London for the JAL meeting.

The JAL meeting seemed a bit ceremonial except for the discussion about a policy dealing with advertising in case of an airline incident irrespective of the company and location. Unfortunately, that policy had to be employed a few times during the 1970s. JAL was among our smallest accounts, using standardized advertising created and coordinated by Ketchum International in various markets. In Iran, we were focusing on the airline's inflight service featuring Japanese kimono-wearing flight attendants.

Triumph 70, one of the largest and most glamorous European fashion shows, came to Tehran around that time. The show featured what they called foundation garments for women. I oversaw promotions of the event in Tehran, as well as the logistics and the preparations for the show at the Tehran Hilton Ballroom. The theme song was "Happy Days," and the focus was on women's beauty, sexuality, and freedom. When the time came to show the line of swimsuits, the stage was flooded with blue lights depicting ocean waves while the models, wearing two-piece swimsuits, made swimming motions. Everyone was impressed with the show and afterward, the client told me that several models/dancers wanted to see Tehran and asked whether I would be willing to show them around the next day. There were about nine girls who wanted to go on the tour. I asked one of our young assistants at the agency to go with me; there were five in my car and four in his. The women wanted to see some exotic places in Tehran so my colleague suggested we go to the famous 16-story Plasco building where there was a hookah lounge that the girls might like.

Plasco was an iconic landmark and one of the tallest in Iran at the time. It belonged to Habib Elghanian, a prominent businessman who was the head of Tehran Jewish Association—after the 1979 Islamic Revolution, Shia clerics tried and executed him. On the building's ground floor, there was a hookah lounge with glass doors and a glass wall on the foyer side. When they saw the hookahs, they got excited and started smoking. After about 10 minutes, I looked back at the foyer side and saw a mob of men—old and young—trying to cross a line of three baton-wielding policemen to get to the glass wall to see the women, who were wearing jeans and light tops, smoking. It was so new to them and they were curious. Some had already made it and were squishing their faces on the glass. I wish I had brought a camera as it was probably the funniest scene. The crowd extended to the street and it looked like we were soon going to have real riot. With the help of a few policemen, we managed to extricate the models and take them to the Tehran Grand Bazar, which was a lot safer, and they bought souvenirs. Unfortunately, the historic Plasco building was destroyed by fire in 2017.

In the summer of 1971, I was looking for a long-term relationship. In Iran, people worked half day on Thursdays and since Fridays were holidays, most social events took place on Thursday evenings. One Thursday evening, I was invited to a party by a cousin who was completing her last year at Farah Women University, an all-girl school, to meet a few of her university friends. It was an exciting opportunity and I met four or five of her classmates, one of the girls was accompanied by her teenage brother. They told me they were heading to the Gol Restaurant, a cozy romantic restaurant with dancing that often had a live band. It was located on the top floor of the famous Aluminum Building, another iconic Tehran building that belonged to Elghanian. I decided to go with the group; as the only man in the group, my odds looked pretty good. I was hoping to get to know some of the girls and have a few dances that evening.

There were a lot of policemen and special security personnel there because a special government fundraising event for the refugees Saddam Hussein had deported from Iraq was going on and some television cameras were inside the restaurant. This was not quite what I had expected but could not back out. Unfortunately, there was a hefty cover charge and, except for my cousin who had received a ticket from where she worked, we had no tickets. It was customary in Iran for men to pay so I had to buy tickets for everyone if I wanted to see any of them again. We were the only young group there that had several attractive young females. We were seated at a round table right in front of the stage. Speaker after speaker angrily denounced Saddam Hussein for his brutal treatment of Iranian people in his country. By that time, a chunk of my salary was already gone with little prospects of having a conversation or dancing with anyone. Older men who looked like army officers in civilian clothing were there, probably ordered to attend the government political gathering against Iraq.

I was totally bored and decided to go to the bar and have a drink and the teenager accompanying his sister followed me to the bar. There was no age limit for drinking alcohol in Iran. I ordered a carafe of Balsam, the local vodka, which came with the customary bowl of cooked pinto beans. I noticed the young man was drinking fast and ate all the beans. When we got back to the table, the TV camera was close and getting shots of the young women. As soon as we sat down, the young man stood up and, as if hypnotized, started shooting pinto beans like a machine gun from his mouth in all directions, accompanied by several loud burps. Beans pelted the faces and heads of our tablemates and several stuck to the TV camera. It was so embarrassing that I abruptly got up and headed toward the exit with the young guy was following me. This was not the kind of event that you would leave early and a police officer at the door asked me if there was anything wrong. I told him my friend was not feeling well but the teenager said he was feeling fine although he could not even stand up straight.

As the officer looked at me suspiciously, the small nearby elevator—with a nice mirror right across the door—opened. We made our way to the elevator with the officer very close to us. The young man mistook the mirror for a window and turned toward it; with a loud burp, several pinto beans leaped from his mouth and slid down the mirror. Fortunately, the elevator door closed before we were arrested for disturbing the peace at a government-sponsored event, which carried a severe punishment.

The week after the Gol Restaurant fiasco, my Aunt Behi, who was like a sister to me, invited me and my cousin Shahram to a birthday party for a university friend of hers. After dinner, I noticed a girl and her classmates on the other side of the room. She caught my eye, and I am not sure how it happened, but we were soon dancing. Sherry was completing her last year as a psychology major at Farah University. Her classes were in the evening, and she taught at an elementary school during the day. She had previously attended the University of Tehran and studied literature for a year but switched to psychology at Farah University where she got the top score in the entrance examination.

After the party, I gave her a ride to her home, which was close to my house on Roosevelt Avenue. I also gave her my phone number, hoping she would call me. A couple of days later, she called, and we had our first date. I picked her up from her university and we went to a romantic restaurant in a basement on Takhte Tavous Avenue. I told her my story and we had dinner and a bottle of wine, dancing after we had discussed and resolved all the world's issues. After the four-hour date, I felt very different. I was anxious to see her again and I knew this was going to be a long-term relationship. Indeed, it has lasted half a century so far. Sherry is attractive, intelligent, educated, and modest. She was well received by my parents and her parents liked me. We got married a couple of years later.

In November of 1972, I was invited to visit Matsushita Electrical Industrial in Japan, one of the world's largest producers of electrical products and marketing under National and Panasonic brand names. I was handling advertising and public relations for the National group of products, including a popular rice cooker and television sets in Iran. I also was eager to visit their agency, Dentsu Advertising, the largest in the world. I got a permit to travel abroad and Mr. Kageyama, the Japanese representative of the National brand in Iran, organized a program in Tokyo and Osaka during my stay in Japan.

I arrived in Tokyo late and checked into the New Otani Hotel. In the elevator, I noticed two kimono-wearing ladies facing the elevator and performing synchronized bows of respect as the elevator doors were closing, something I had never seen in Iran or any other country. On our way to Dentsu Advertising the next day, I told the representative that it seemed men were quite dominant in Japan. He smiled and told me what I saw at the elevator was just a show of respect to hotel customers and, in fact, women had a lot more power than men in the household. At Dentsu, I met some young and very sharp people who were part of the group handling the National and Panasonic brand accounts. They showed me some of their commercials; they were nicely done but were mostly symbolic using family, nature and traditional scenes. There were many long shots showing a group of people or background scenes with implicit and indirect messages. They were so different from the European commercials that were like mini movies with stylistic sets designed more for entertainment. Japanese commercials were also different from American commercials that were more straightforward, using explicit messages with a strong focus on individuals, and packed with information.

Another point of contrast with the US advertising was that Dentsu handled our competitors like Toshiba, Sharp, and Hitachi among others, under the same roof. American companies were especially sensitive about their agencies handling competitors. They told me that even opposing political candidates use the same advertising agencies in Japan.

That evening, I met with the Iranian partners of the company for a buffet dinner at the Otani Hotel Sky revolving restaurant. The Tokyo view was stunning and the food was great. I went for seconds and thirds, but the older gentlemen just ate a little for health reasons. We discussed the most significant technological advancement in television manufacturing in Iran— the moving from lamp television sets to the transistor ones. We wanted to use our successful national variety television show to convey the benefits of transistor TV sets to our audiences in small towns. People's knowledge of television technology was quite limited; some people would check the quality of a TV set by putting their child on the television cabinet to see if it was strong enough before purchasing it.

The next day, a guy from Dentsu Advertising and I took the famous bullet train to Osaka, the second largest city in Japan, where Matsushita Industrial Headquarters were located. We visited the Matsushita Museum and learned that its still-living founder, Mr. Matsushita Konosuke, started the company in 1918 by producing lightbulbs and sockets and had made it among the largest electronic companies in the world. I noticed that people at Matsushita were working extra hard, even after hours, for no overtime pay and just modest salaries. Everyone was wearing a simple, gray uniform and before work every morning, each unit had an in-person meeting.

The company had an interesting publication, *PHP*, "Peace, Happiness through Prosperity." Mr. Matsushita was credited for introducing a decentralized management system in the American tradition where each unit could make autonomous decisions under the overall coordination of the central management. This was probably quite innovative in a county where the management style had been always hierarchical, from top to bottom. My Japanese colleague said that many companies were trying to relocate to Tokyo to enjoy the proximity to the government, which played a large role in the private sector and export subsidies. It seemed to me that building relationships and trust came before business transactions in Japan. The Dentsu people took me out to fancy dinners and many entertainment night spots and we became friends. I also felt that Iran was achieving much credibility and respect in the world.

In Tokyo, I visited a direct mail house and learned about its operation and business model. With the help of a couple of friends, Ali and John, I created the first direct marketing company in Iran on the side. Our very first client, our agency client, was Japan Airlines. We took over their mailings as well as their equipment that consisted of an addressograph and metal plates. Soon, we got an order from another client, Proctor & Gamble, promoting their detergent Tide in Tehran with a large mailing. This was a huge opportunity. We bought a device to copy address labels from paper cards, but addresses in Tehran were irregular—some were like giving mini directions and most people had their names on their doors. We decided to hire high school students to go house to house to physically collect the addresses and placed a couple of employment ads in a newspaper. The response was overwhelming since there were not many work opportunities for high schoolers during summer. We hired many students and two secretaries typed the addresses on the special machine cards. Everything was going smoothly until one of the student workers went to the home of a high-ranking officer of SAVAK, the country's dreaded secret police, and insisted on getting the name of the person living there since, understandably, there was no nameplate on the door. He was arrested and released, but I was summoned to Tehran's police headquarters.

I was directed to a hallway where two large doors were shut behind me. In a room of about 15 people, a man interrogated me. I showed him our brochure but it was in English and he couldn't read it. My explanations were useless as he knew nothing about marketing or advertising. He suspiciously kept asking why we were collecting addresses before finally leaving the room with our brochures. I noticed a bunch of forms on his desk with a blank for a name, followed by a line saying something to the effect that this person acted against the national security of the country. I was getting scared and asked one of the people in the room if I could call my lawyer but he said that no lawyers were allowed there. A man carrying small glasses of tea on a tray occasionally came to the room and offered tea to everyone except me. When the interrogator returned, he signaled the tea man to give me tea, which seemed to indicate that I was off the hook. He warned me to stop the practice since the list could fall into the wrong hands and the company may be held responsible. That was the end of our direct mail company in Iran.

One of the most exciting projects that I had in the early 1970s was producing the *National Show*, a one-hour weekly variety television show sponsored by the National brand for promoting Matsushita's National products, especially its new transistor television sets. The popular show was watched by millions in Iran and in some parts of neighboring countries. We had three minutes for commercials before and after the show, which was taped before a live audience. We gave away National rice cookers, transistor radios, and TV sets as prizes to winners as another way to promote our products. The National people wanted Ali Tabesh, a popular actor and comedian—albeit old school—to host the show. Most Iranian bands and singers accepted our invitation without hesitation. Female singers frequently asked me how they looked on camera while singing. NIRT people assigned a very capable female director and I developed a good rapport with her, but her crew often stopped at critical moments to take a break or go to dinner.

A former radio announcer, Mr. Mani, had a supervisory role for content, but his main work for us was censorship. I had to submit a detailed account of the entire show's format and content each week before taping but he was often explosive and abused his authority.

Many people wanted to obtain tickets to watch the show in the studio. After a while, we replaced Ali Tabesh with Fereydoun Farrokhzad, a very popular singer and comedian, to appeal to younger audiences. Part of his initial name recognition was due to his sister, Forugh Farrokhzad, an avant-garde and extremely popular poet who had died in a car accident at the age of 32. She was a feminist poet, and her expressions were explicit and direct, yet soft and sensual from the perspective of a woman. She was way ahead of her time in a traditional Iranian society.

As part of repackaging the show, we decided to produce a fancy introduction film. I took Farrokhzad—an openly gay man, unique in Iran—to the Cinegraphic Studio for a shoot. I could not believe how most of the otherwise conservative women stopped to watch him or wave at him; some were even sending him kisses. We had a few near misses with cars that came too close to say hello to him. He was extremely popular, but as is the case with a lot of creative people, Farrokhzad was not easy to work with. On set one day while giving a National rice cooker as a prize, he incorrectly said that it worked off battery power too. For some reason, the crew was unable to change that so the day after the broadcast we faced a crisis; dealers from all over the country were sending the electric rice cookers back and asking for the battery-powered ones since Iranian consumers wanted to cook fresh rice on picnics. Of course, no such rice cooker existed. The show was so popular that even after National discontinued its sponsorship, it was renamed *Mikhak-e-Noghr-e-ee* (silver carnation) and continued by the NIRT. After the 1979 Islamic Revolution, Farrokhzad became a major critic of the Islamic regime and Ayatollah Khomeini, using humor, irony and sarcasm. In 1992, Farrokhzad was assassinated in his apartment in Bon, Germany.

Meanwhile, Sherry and I were serious about each other. She graduated and worked as a counselor at an all-girl high school but complained that some students were smoking cigarettes, had boyfriends, and wore quite a bit of makeup in school— but cleaned up before going home. One day, she invited me to the school for an event held in the schoolyard, and many parents attended. Sherry was one of the speakers and delivered an impressive talk in her pleasant voice. We had a wonderful relationship, but I was not ready for marriage. I knew she was under pressure from her traditional family to get married and I didn't want to stand in her way should she want to do that. I finally told her that I was not ready for marriage and continuing our relationship may not be the best option for her. That was so hard for me. Tears streamed down her face as I spoke. She left and later told me that she cried all night but in the morning she decided to forget me.

We had not seen each other for eight months, and I was missing her. She was not teaching anymore and had been transferred to the office of exceptional children where they oversaw standardizing aptitude and IQ tests in Iran but I did not know where her office was. I was having lunch with an American client one day who had brought along an American friend that told me he was in Iran to help standardize a series of aptitude and other tests. I asked him if he knew Ms. Shahin (Sherry) Tavassoli. He said yes and that her boss was planning to marry her. I felt like I had been hit by a truck. I should have expected her to get married sometime, but I was surprised by my reaction after hearing the news. He told me where their office was so the next day, I went to Sherry's office and took her to lunch in the backyard of my parents' house. Under a sleeping willow tree, she told me that she had no interest in her boss. I asked her if she would marry me. She held my hand and said yes. I talked to her father, Ali Tavassoli, a very nice man who told me that if I wanted Sherry, I should marry her soon. As was customary, a couple of days later, my mother and I went to their house with a nice bouquet of roses. I met her two brothers and two sisters. Her mother was not very happy about it but we set a date: September 12, 1973.

The next step was to take Sherry, her mother, Touran, and her rich aunt, Pary, to visit jewelry shops to select a ring for Sherry. I had not realized how expensive weddings were; the ones her mother and aunt liked had astronomical price tags. While they were looking and discussing various rings, Sherry and

I went to another shop and bought a nice diamond ring for a reasonable price.

We decided we wanted to have an intimate, cozy wedding reception. We planned to have our ceremony in Sherry's bedroom and the reception on the large terrace of her parents' house. I asked a family friend to perform the formal ceremony and recording. Based on the traditional Iranian custom, the groom pays the wedding expenses, and as part of the marriage document, he commits to a certain sum in gold or local currency, payable to the bride on demand. The bride supplies all the household items needed for starting a new life together as her dowry. Sherry took me to a branch of the ministry of education co-op store where there were all types of nice furniture and household items. We bought everything we needed for a small monthly payment deducted from Sherry's government salary.

On the day of our wedding, I went to the Nemooneh Barbershop, owned by Agha Taghi. He had been giving me haircuts for years. I remember Agha Taghi working as an assistant in the barbershop when I was in high school, but when I got back from the US, he was the owner. He was a simple, hardworking man. As time went on, he expanded his shop and installed sinks for shampooing. Soon, he was serving Turkish coffee, and a woman was telling my fortune by reading the lines created in the bottom of the coffee cup while I was getting a haircut. He also built a mezzanine type room for breaks. A couple of years after my wedding, he was seldom there. One day, an employee told me he was upstairs gambling. Soon, there was a small advertisement in the paper announcing the change of title of his shop, and he went back to being the assistant again. He lost his life's work to gambling. I was so sorry for him.

Our wedding was a bit rushed. We invited family members and close friends to the reception and dinner. During the ceremony, we both sat behind a *sofreh aghd* (wedding table) beautifully decorated with mirrors, herbs, pastries, honey, frankincense, and so on. Persian wedding ceremonies go back to the Zoroastrian era, a pre-Islamic ancient Persian religion founded by Zoroaster in the sixth century, BC. Our ceremony was a watered-down version of that. Some families insist on following every ritual detail before, during, and after the wedding. During the ceremony, the official reads the entire marriage document twice and asks for the bride but the bride remains silent and family members say she has gone to pick flowers. After a third reading, she finally says yes, consenting to the marriage. Men answer yes after the first time. We both signed the official record book together with the two required witnesses, my father and hers. The next step was lifting her veil and seeing her face in the mirror; according to some, it signifies the eternity of love and marriage. Then, the famous Persian song *Mobarak Bad* (Congratulations) was played. I lifted the bowl of honey and dipped my pinky in it then put it in Sherry's mouth, and she did the same, symbolizing the idea that we would feed each other sweetness as we began our lives together. Our immediate family members kissed us and congratulated us in addition to giving gifts before we took a break and prepared for the reception.

The weather was very nice that evening and it felt great to see all our family and friends having a good time and wishing us well. My mom and Sherry's father worked very hard that night to make sure that everything went smoothly. Everyone was dancing and Ali made a nice little 16 mm film from the wedding. Unfortunately, we had a lousy photographer and the wedding pictures did not turn out well. After the wedding, I drove Sherry to our new home as our family members drove behind us in the streets of Tehran. They honked in jubilation while following us to the new home, a customary celebratory expression. Only the bedroom of the luxury apartment we had rented was fully furnished. Except for a refrigerator in which my mom left a bottle of champagne and some snacks, the rest of the furniture had not yet been delivered. We had quite a few parties for family and friends, and they brought all kinds of gifts, from heaters to cocktail tables and crystal glasses to china sets.

Toward the mid-1970s, I was an account supervisor with three account executives and a couple of assistants at Caspian Advertising, but my growth in that agency had reached its limit. Most of my time was spent on educating our prospective clients, thinking of new ideas, and making presentations. It came to me naturally. I was offered several nice positions, including sales manager for the National brand in Iran and marketing manager for Bristol Myers in Iran. Admen Advertising was a successful advertising agency headed by Tony. Tony had asked me a couple of times to join him and offered a much larger salary. Hamideh Azodi, known as Hamoush, was the main investor of Admen Advertising. The story was that after leaving Caspian Inc., Tony and John had persuaded Colgate Palmolive and Esso, a brand of Exxon, to move their accounts to the new agency. Hamoush, a socialite and a princess from Qajar dynasty that ruled Iran before the Pahlavi's, took interest in the new Admen Advertising agency. Her husband, the legendary oil and gas pipeline engineer Ian Bowler, had a contract with the National Iranian Oil Company (AIOC) to lay oil and gas pipes. He designed and constructed a one-thousand-mile gas pipeline that stretched from Ahwaz, close to the Persian Gulf, to Astara, the Soviet border town on the Caspian Sea. The $800 million pipeline was an engineering marvel rising fourteen thousand feet over the Zagros Mountains that covered the length of Iran. Hamoush provided the necessary capital for the start of the new company and became a nominal board member, although the Admen Advertising venture was just a hobby for her and the investment was chump change.

Hamoush invited me to visit her one afternoon. She and her husband lived in a large luxury home with a huge backyard. When I entered the house, I was greeted by two hyper German shepherds. A massive tent stood in the backyard for holding large receptions. Hamoush graciously introduced me to her husband, Mr. Bowler, as a rising advertising star in Iran. She offered me the position of executive director of the company with 10 percent equity in the company plus an annual salary of around $50K—a considerable figure in early 1974 Iran. Ms. Azodi impressed me and, despite my loyalty to Caspian Advertising and Dr. Abdoli, I felt it was about time to move on. I accepted the offer. The company was well known among international companies in Tehran with solid clients such as Bristol Myers, Colgate Palmolive, and Exxon, mainly because of Tony's strong sense of enterprise and his interpersonal communication skills with American and British clients. Tony arranged meetings with me and his major clients and they all were quite encouraging.

In 1974, the International Advertising Association Conference was held in Tehran. The government went all-out to impress the advertising world, especially American and British delegates and several cabinet members hosted glamorous receptions. The Iranian chapter had a great showing in membership numbers but it did not really reflect the size and prestige of the advertising industry at that time. I attended most events but did not hear a single Iranian researcher discussing advertising and marketing in Iran. I attended a plenary speech by an American psychologist about the future attitudes of American college students. She predicted that unlike the 1970s rebels, the next generation of college students would respect the establishment, be brand-loyal, and aspire to be hired by corporate America. Their appearance would be conservative and they would like to marry and have children. It turned out that her predictions were absolutely accurate.

After working at Admen Advertising for several months, I started to find ways of improving our services, making the agency operations more efficient and helping expand our client base in the face of declining profit margins due to the hyperinflation. Tony frequently traveled abroad and I soon became the managing director of the company. Hamoush supported me and sometimes helped our public relations by organizing receptions at her beautiful home.

A rather strange event happened in 1975 when Rudy Kishazy, who introduced himself as a world champion in hang gliding, visited me. He was planning to jump off Mount Damavand, the highest peak in Iran and the highest volcano listed in Asia. He mentioned that NIRT had already agreed to film his jump from a helicopter. He wanted us to help him put together the film and market it internationally, especially in the UK and the US, through our advertising contacts. We came across a lot of proposals like that so I did not take it seriously at first. Rudy told us that he was training General Khatami, the brother-in-law of and advisor to the shah as well as the commander of the Iranian Imperial Air Force. Later, we heard that the TV cameras malfunctioned and could not film the jump. A week or so later, General Khatami was mysteriously killed in a hang-gliding accident. After the general's death, Rudy suggested that he may have encountered a heavy wind gust that he could not control. This was about four years before the Islamic Revolution; afterward, there were many conspiracy theories about the general's death.

In the fall 1974, Sherry was starting to feel nauseated, especially around cooked meat. Yes, she was pregnant, and we became busy preparing the baby's room—the crib, furniture, clothing, and toys; it was a wonderful time. When she was close to delivery, I took her to Tehran Clinic, an upscale hospital in Tehran where the doctor told her that she needed a Cesarean section. We were hesitant and got a second opinion, and Mike Farbod Zandpour was born by C-section in March of 1975. He was the most handsome baby in the entire maternity ward, with thick, dark eyelashes and shiny black hair. I took a large, beautiful bouquet of red roses and a gold necklace to Sherry in the hospital. It was a joy to take the baby home. When I married Sherry, my life space expanded to include her as well, but when Mike was born, my lifetime was extended beyond my own to include Mike.

It was an amazing feeling! I normally got home when Mike was asleep but was in the habit of getting up several times during the night to check whether he was breathing. A few days after Mike was born, I had a lunch meeting at a high-end restaurant with the Bristol Myers people. When the general manager, an Italian man named Mr. Botticelli, heard I had just become a father, he treated everyone to champagne and cigars. It was a nice gesture that I really appreciated.

I had found my calling in advertising and was making serious money, especially after 1974 when the oil embargo quadrupled the price from $3 to $12 per barrel. I was also feeling that by introducing new and innovative products, I was contributing to improving the standard of living of the Iranian people. The country was awash with cash when bottlenecks started to congest ports and roads. A construction boom led many people to leave their villages and agricultural work for more lucrative construction jobs in urban areas, especially Tehran. Inflation was rampant and there was much displacement and frustration.

In 1975, there was no apparent sign of dissent or anti-shah demonstrations. Islamic clerics were ostensibly either in support of the shah's regime or in jail. The middle class was enjoying the newfound income from the country's increased oil revenues and was busy emulating Western lifestyles. There were, however, subtle indications that all was not well. The shah occasionally talked about the unholy alliance of black and red conspiring against him—Islamic Marxists; black indicated Muslim militants, and red referred to Marxists. From time to time, we saw Parviz Sabeti, introduced on national television during prime time as a security authority, discuss the arrests of who they called destructionists. He also displayed a large cache of arms that had been seized. Chief among the destructionists, they said, were People's Fedayeen, introduced as a Marxist guerrilla group, and People's Mujaheddin, a hybrid Islamic and Marxist group. It seemed little attention was paid to conservative militant Islamists.

At the height of Iran's economic growth, the shah closed all traditional political parties in Iran, which I thought was one of his most egregious mistakes during his reign. By replacing existing political parties with a single party, he deprived the country of public debates and the marketplace of ideas to solve the deep problems that were emerging from rapid social and economic changes. Prior to 1975, the two major political parties in Iran were Mardom (people) and Iran Novin (the new Iran). The latter was the shah's party promoting his White Revolution policies aiming at modernizing Iran. But in 1975, the shah banned all political parties and founded a single party, Rastakihiz-e-Iran (Iran's resurrection party), based on three principles: the monarchy regime, the revolution of the Shah and the nation, and the Iranian constitution.

He forced all business associations to create a party chapter to educate the business community about the goals of the new party. There was also a youth Ratsakhiz section.

Farhad Hormozi organized the chapter of the party for our business association. As the owner and president of Faccoupa Advertising and with Blite Bakht Azmai (Iranian national lottery)—and its massive advertising budgets—as its sole client, he was the de facto leader of Iranian advertising. Every Wednesday, the lottery was drawn with much fanfare and billions of rials in prizes were announced on national media. Tickets were issued by the agency *Eaneh Meli* (National Contributions) that was overseen by Princess Asharf Pahlavi, the twin sister of the shah of Iran. Hormozi was an influential figure in the advertising industry, mainly because of his connection with the princess and the huge advertising budget he controlled.

As the first step in organizing our industry's chapter, Hormozi rented a house in northern Tehran with a large room and conference table for our monthly meetings. The shah's dictatorial style was emulated in every level of the government and the private sector all the way to families and Hormozi was no exception. About 30 people showed up during the first meeting and were all advertising or media executives. Hormozi always sat at the head of the table and ran the meeting like a dictator. The first meeting was chaotic at times without anything like *Robert's Rules of Order*. People started talking over each other with long lists of complaints about the government, economy, clients, and employees. A few were upset and left the meeting for not being able to finish their thoughts, but Hormozi eventually took the control of the meeting. A couple of months later when Hormozi was absent, the meeting was in a shambles with several unrelated arguments taking place across the table among competing advertising agencies. The concept of public debate for a country that had been run authoritatively for centuries was strange, not to mention that most men present were authoritarian in their own rights. That day, I could not help but think about the fate of the country if something happened to the shah.

During mid-1970s, our company was benefiting from a constant stream of Americans and Europeans passing through Iran as they were traveling the world. We hired some who had experience in advertising, albeit on a temporary basis. They always brought in fresh perspectives and our clients liked the practice. I think the first one was Gilbert, a French guy; Scott, a Dutch; and the next was Mark, a British guy who loved to play squash. At that time, there was only one squash court in Tehran and it was exclusively for members of the Bank-e-Sepah Club. We became members and regularly played there, mainly on Thursday afternoons. My father said that I should have some type of eye protection. I tried to find goggles without success and thought my dad was a bit old and too conservative.

A family member had married Jeff, an American who worked in the oil and gas field in Aghajari, an oil town south of Iran, who loved to play squash too. One afternoon, I was doing well toward the end of the last game and had a great shot, but after a few seconds, I didn't hear anything and turned my head to encounter what felt like a truck hitting me. The ball struck me at top speed and threw me to the floor. I felt tremendous pain in my eye. As Jeff was trying to help me out of the building, he ruptured a tendon and was in great pain. Someone gave us a ride to the Jam Hospital where they told us they had no eye specialist. Our ride had left, so with great difficulty, we reached the Tehran Clinic Hospital. An eye specialist saw and admitted me to the hospital without doing anything. Jeff was admitted too, and our rooms were next to each other. I was in so much pain that night. The doctor performed surgery the next morning to relieve the pressure that had already caused major damage. He was teaching an assistant while he was doing surgery on my eye. When they returned me to my room, my family was there; Sherry was hiding her tears and it was the first time that I saw my dad cry. It could go either way.

The instrument for measuring the interocular pressure was awkward. Dr. Rice had performed surgery on my younger cousin Shane so Sherry went to the university to get a letter to start the process I had used before for traveling to England. She was informed that since I had graduated, the university could no longer issue a letter that I was studying there. This was very bad news, adding insult to injury. I was not able to use the procedure to go abroad and would soon be drafted.

As luck would have it, my aunt's husband came to visit me at the hospital the next evening with his friend who was an eye specialist. The friend said that he knew the general who oversaw eye examinations for military service exemptions. He could use his connection with the general but was not sure how fast they could get the committee together. I called our old neighbor General Shayanfar who had helped me with my travel before and he told me he would let me know the next day. That evening, I saw Mike after I had been in the hospital for a few weeks. He had just learned to walk and gave a bunch of small flowers. I was so happy to see him and so sad that I could not get up and hug him.

General Shayanfar told me the committee would see me that day. This spoke to the general's power, since the committee consisted of a group of senior military officers and getting all those important people together on short notice was tough. After examining my eye, they gave me a temporary exemption to go abroad for medical reasons and said that when I returned, I should take the documents to the conscription office and have them signed by a general in charge for permanent military exemption. My secretary, a young Armenian lady, arranged for Sherry and me to travel. On the ride to the airport, Mike sat on Sherry's lap and looked at my eyepatch with a sad face. He knew something bad had happened and that we were going to leave him soon. Sherry told me to hold his hand, which I did for the first time ever, and I immediately felt the connection. It was something I had never experienced before.

Sherry had dealt with my situation for about a month and was taking her first trip ever out of the country. When we checked into our London hotel room, she lay on the bed and started crying, decompressing in a strange place with a huge problem. The next day, we saw Dr. Rice at his office on Harley Street. The first thing he did was take off my eyepatch and ask for my eye medication, both of which he threw into the waste basket. After that, I felt calm. He thoroughly examined my eye and told me I had a thick blood clot in my eye; there was a 50 percent chance that it would be absorbed over time. He also told me (correctly) that I would eventually develop cataracts. He gave me some medication and asked me to see him in 10 days.

After being in the hospital for three weeks, I had lost weight and felt weak, but psychologically, I was boosted by the doctor's positive remarks. When we got back to our hotel, by sheer coincidence, we saw one of Sherry's best friends from college. Vida was with her husband and son visiting Vida's brother in Folkstone in southeast England. They invited us to share the house that they had rented for a month or so by the English Channel; we could have the downstairs room if we wanted. We gladly accepted. The house was a waterfront two-story building with large windows and a gorgeous view of the Channel. At night, the waves crashed on the window of our room. Upstairs on a clear night, we could see the lights of Calais, France, which was about 30 minutes by hovercrafts from nearby Dover.

We had been sitting in the sun in a park near our house in Folkston when I noticed a group of teenagers riding their bikes and playing. One of them showed us a piece of paper and asked if it was ours. The paper had been in Sherry's wallet inside her purse in the car. The place was considered so safe that most people left their cars unlocked. Her wallet and all the Iranian money in it had been stolen, but the travelers' checks and British pounds were still in her purse. When Sherry told him how badly we needed the prescription for my eye medication, the boy suggested that we follow him into a wooded area. I initially refused and didn't want Sherry to go either, but she did and found my prescription among her purse's scattered contents. When we returned home, I called the police and reported the incident. A policeman came by the house and took a report. We didn't think anything would come out of it.

The next day, we all took a trip from Dover to Calais by hovercraft then a train to Paris. When we returned after a few days of sightseeing in Paris, we had a surprise visitor: the same policeman who had taken our theft report told us that he found our money. He gave us a piece of paper that we were to take to the bank to get the equivalent of Iranian currency in British pounds. We were all amazed at the efficiency of Folkstone police. I invited him to come in for a beer and he did. He was a nice gentleman.

I saw Dr. Rice a few times and he mentioned that I should see him in a couple of months. We visited several historic English sites near Folkstone, including Dover Castle and the Canterbury Cathedral. I was surprised to see so much English heritage in that part of the country. The day before we returned, we visited Hyde Park and had dinner at the Serpentine restaurant. I was slowly getting my energy back and was missing Mike a lot, especially when I saw little boys his age playing in Hyde Park.

When I returned to the office in Tehran after a long period of recuperation, the company was in shambles. Clients were complaining about the poor service and billings had declined. The local distributor of the German AEG home appliances was taking advantage of our situation and asking to lower our commission to five percent. Accepting his request would have significantly damaged the reputation of our company. Other agencies had taken advantage of my absence and were trying to take pieces of our major accounts. To safeguard our company's reputation, I dropped the AEG account right before the Nowruz holiday when he needed advertising the most.

I heard AEG was unable to find any agency to handle their account; I believe major agencies like Caspian, Inc. and Ziba Advertising were already handling home appliance companies that competed directly with AEG. The smaller agencies could not help either since AEG required a substantial credit line with NIRT and since the AEG local agent was notorious—like many Iranian companies—for paying advertising bills with six-month promissory notes. The week following my return, I had lunch with most of our clients and assured them of our continuing quality service. Tony had taken a long vacation to Europe as usual, and the other two partners did not know how to run the agency. Tony ignored my several warnings about not showing up to work, so I fired him. I hired Alan Cordier, an Englishman, as an account executive and offered him double the salary that he was making at Mr. Arbabi's advertising agency. Allan's wife, Mina Bina, was Sherry's Farah University college friend. Mina's sister, Sima Bina, was a popular folk singer. Alan later went to work for Bristol Myers and then Kent Cigarettes. In 2022, I heard his two grown sons are in the advertising business in Iran.

Women were increasingly becoming major purchasers and decision-makers for many products and services in Iran and were therefore featured in most television commercials. Women were making serious advances in television, film, and music, but we had quite a bit of difficulty in finding female models for our shampoo, deodorant, and toothpaste commercials. For the launch of Mum deodorant, we made our commercials in Greece. We also started to film our commercials in London. The local production didn't quite match up to European and American standards. I worked with Drummond Challis, a producer who worked with film director Tony Maylam. Their claim to fame was a documentary film about 1976 Winter Olympics bobsledding in Austria but they were willing to film some commercials in London during their downtime.

I soon went to London for surgery at Wellington Hospital to relieve my eye pressure. The hospital was super luxurious with an extensive menu. I noticed there were Arabic signs in the corridors, the effect of petrodollars, as the price of oil had recently quadrupled. When I had recovered, I went to Samuelson Film Services near Ealing in West London to see Drummond, a Cambridge University graduate who had gotten his training at Samuelson Film Services. We talked about a romantic Mum deodorant commercial that I had in mind in which a couple rode in a carriage through Trafalgar Square at night. Drummond was sharp and got the idea, and I sent him the storyboard when I went back to Iran. The commercial was a total success. We also made a few full-page magazine color print ads from the film scenes.

It was the beginning of a nice partnership with Drummond and Tony Maylam and the production of several successful commercials. On my next trip to London, Tony invited me to dinner. We rode in his fancy sports car and I felt silly for wearing a tie. Tony became a famous British film director, and so did Drummond, who produced many movies. Sydney Samuelson established Samuelson Film Services in 1954 and became the first British film commissioner and was knighted in 1995.

We usually sold a concept to our client by presenting the entire campaign with storyboards and layouts. We had an excellent art director, Ardash, who often worked with his team into the night to prepare the visuals for our presentations. After the client's initial approval, we sent the storyboards to London for a cost estimate. Upon the clients' approval, I took a flight to London to select the talent, normally from a long list of candidates who went to Samuelson Film Services for a standard audition. I left the rest for Drummond to handle. After the shoot, I took the raw 35 mm negatives back to Iran and the Cinegraphic Studio to have it developed at Badii Studio, the only one in Tehran that could reliably do the job. Then, the editing was done based on the storyboard on a machine called Moviola. Once the final version was approved by the client, the rush copy was marked for the cuts, dissolves, and superimpositions, and other transitions. They cut the negatives at Badii Studio and prepared the final copy for client approval before distribution to the media. Unfortunately, the edits did not always come out as precisely as indicated on the rush copy. There is a world of difference from how they edited then and on the fly in 2020s using a computer with Premier, Final Cut Pro, and other software.

The launch of Clairol Great Body shampoo was problematic. The client wanted us to use the commercial shown in the US where several underwater ballerinas pointed out the fact that the shampoo replenished the vital elements that they lose daily in the water. Iranian women could not identify with underwater ballerinas and the commercial and the product was a huge failure. Every time I visited their offices, there were complaints from salesmen that Iran wasn't ready for the non-egg shampoo. Erick Peterson, Bristol's marketing manager, was getting nervous and there was a possibility of moving the account elsewhere. I decided to do a series of phone interviews with women, like what I had done for Triumph International. From the telephone directory, I called random numbers between nine and noon and introduced myself as working at a shampoo factory and asked what women were looking for in a shampoo. All—without exception—said that shampoo must improve the feel and appearance of their hair; the word in Persian is *halat*. We had to decide fast so I looked at a few of Bristol's US commercials and picked one that was called "Shampoo nuts!" We made a 20-second black-and-white commercial with some edits and completely changed the audio where a woman said something like 'Every shampoo cleans my hair, but what is the use; clean with no look and no feel?' The commercial was a miraculous success. Soon, Bristol sold all inventory and was desperately running behind orders due to lack of bottles and caps.

I had saved quite a bit and was ready to buy a house in Tehran's super-expensive real estate market! I suggested that my parents sell their old house and that we buy a nice house with two separate units so that we could live together, and yet separately. We had seen a house in Farmanieh area in Shemiran for a little more than the equivalent of $300,000 US, an average price for a middle-class house at that time in Tehran. It was a new, two-story house with three bedrooms on each floor, a living and dining room, kitchen, and two bathrooms that overlooked a nice garden in one of the best areas close to the shah's Niavaran Palace. I talked with the retired army colonel owner who was a hard bargainer. After a bit of negotiating, we decided to buy the house provided the seller would fix a few things. I gave the owner a check equivalent of about $45,000 US and signed an agreement about what needed to be fixed by a certain date; that's how things were done in those days in Iran.

About a month later, I inspected the house but the seller had not done anything. By then, home prices had gone up a little and he told me if I wasn't happy, he would give me my money back. I accepted and he gave me a check. I gave him a receipt indicating that by cashing the check our agreement about the purchase of the house would be nullified. In the late evening of the same day, he called me at home and said he did not have enough money in that particular account and wanted me to return that check in exchange for a new one the next day. The next day, I had a few important meetings with clients and Sherry had to go to work so I asked my parents, who were taking care of Mike, to make this exchange of checks. I arranged for the exchange to happen inside the Bank-e-Melli (Central Branch of the National Bank) since I knew security was tight, just in case the colonel was planning to pull something funny.

Around noon, Sherry called me and told me that something had gone wrong—my mom was in the police station at *Peech-e-Shemiran*. When my parents and Mike went to the bank and met with the colonel, he asked for the old check. As soon as my mom showed it to him, he grabbed it and tried to eat it! He figured that if he ate the entire check, there would be no evidence and he could keep the house and our $45,000. Even if we took him to civil court, it would be years before the court would look at our case and if we succeeded, our money would be worth a lot less because of the high inflation rate. Fortunately, security saw what the colonel was doing and managed to take a portion of the check from the colonel's mouth, write a police report, and send him to the police station. When I arrived at the police station, the captain in charge told me that the colonel had his own check in his possession and there seemed to be no issue. The colonel's son-in-law, a senior manager at the telephone company, had promised the captain a landline—which was very expensive and hard to get—so the captain wrote a report in favor of the colonel! I was so angry about how they treated my mother and we were all told to go to court near the police station Saturday morning, the first day of the week in Iran.

That Friday, we had a family friend over for lunch. Since he was in real estate, we told him our story and he said that he knew the judge there. Immediately, he called the judge's home and explained the situation. The judge asked to see me first thing on Saturday. I went to the judge's office on the second floor of the courthouse in *Peech-e-Shemiran* and introduced myself. The judge did not say much and asked me to go downstairs and wait. Downstairs, the colonel and his son-in-law appeared quite confident and happy. The colonel was telling people that we had a civil dispute. A young investigator who was constantly playing with his car keys as though he had just bought the car, called us to his desk. He asked the colonel to explain what happened and the colonel stated what he had told the captain in the police precinct. The investigator said his story contradicted what he had told bank security. The colonel replied that he'd had a headache at the time and did not quite remember what he had said. The investigator set the colonel's bail for the check's equivalent and asked a policeman to take the colonel straight to Ghasr Prison. His son-in-law wanted to bring a property deed or cash for bail but it was too late in the day and the investigator was already on another case. After a day or so, the colonel made bail and was released. His long hair had been shaved in Ghasr Prison and he was in deep trouble unless we agreed to drop the charges. Eventually, after giving us another $10,000 discount and fixing all that we had earlier agreed upon, we dropped the charges and soon moved into the new home.

Sherry's father supervised some remodeling in the house; we removed the wall between the dining and the living room, built a nice patio with marble flooring, and remodeled the bathrooms and kitchen. Sherry ordered Italian leather furniture and I brought back a very nice chandelier from London together with colorful wallpaper for Mike's room. My father-in-law installed the chandelier the same night I returned from London. We held so many family parties and get-togethers there! My parents lived upstairs and Sherry's family lived very close on Sabt street in Tajrish. I had swapped my Peugeot 504 for a brand-new maroon Buick Skylark. I bought a bike and helmet for Mike, and we all were extremely happy. I had everything I had wished for!

The company was doing well and we managed to buy Tony's and Hamush Azodi's shares of the company. We were handling a long list of brands from domestic and international clients, including Canada Dry, Colgate Palmolive, ExxonMobil, Bristol Myers, and Tolid Daru.

Singapore Airlines was a small client, but it was fun. I had a good relationship with Mr. Goh, Singapore Airlines' regional manager. Mr. Goh was Malaysian and his elegant wife was from the Emirates. We entertained them at our house a few times and once they brought us real snakeskin as a gift, I got scared just looking at it. The main agency, Batey Ads, had created the Singapore Girl campaign, "A Great Way to Fly." We helped the airline to organize and promote a joint promotion with Singapore's tourist promotion board in Tehran's Hilton Hotel with the theme of Polynesia. We had beautiful Polynesian music, dances, and great food. The Singapore staff seemed quite professional and hardworking. The event was a great success and received much publicity!

When I first visited Singapore to attend the airlines' conference, I couldn't believe how peaceful and harmonious the three distinct ethnic groups—Chinese, Malaysian, and Indian—with different customs and religions were living together. A joke at the conference was that Singapore Airlines made sure three seats in every row of the plane were sold to passengers from one of the three ethnic groups and sat them next to each other. The regional manager Mr. Goh was an ethnic Malay, the president of Singapore Airlines was an ethnic Chinese, Mr. Chan, and the chairman of the airline, Mr. Pillay, was an ethnic Indian.

In the mid-1970s, Iran looked quite stable and relatively prosperous; many foreigners visited Iran to explore business partnerships and investment opportunities. One day, a tall gentleman visited our agency and introduced himself as John R. Thompson, representing BBDO from New York, one of the largest advertising conglomerates in the United States. It was around lunchtime, so I invited him to have lunch with me and our accounting guy. We went to the Polynesian restaurant in the Intercontinental Hotel where we held Christmas parties for our American clients. John said that the main reason for BBDO's interest in Iran was that RJR, a major client of theirs, was planning to expand their activities in Iran. We decided that we would pursue the matter further!

A month later, someone named Ruben from RJR visited us and invited us to an RJR promotional event at a Caspian Sea resort near the city of Chalus. RJR had many products and seemed like a great client. Soon, we met Steve Kahler from BBDO and a colleague of his in London, a financial director at BBDO. We made a presentation about the agency, but contrary to our expectations, most questions during that meeting were not related to finances. BBDO was more interested in learning about us as people, although accounting questions like billings and margins came up. Subsequently, our company was audited by Price Waterhouse in Iran. Willi Schalk, BBDO's vice president of international operations and former managing director of team BBDO Germany, together with John Thompson, visited our agency in Tehran and we signed an agreement for Admen Advertising to become Admen/BBDO with detailed equity and financial arrangements.

The last advertising campaign I ran before the 1979 uprising was for Lyco, a company that made pillows and comforters in Tabriz, a city in the northwestern province of Azerbaijan. The president of the company was a bright young man in his early 30s. He invited me to Tabriz, about an hour away by plane. I was impressed by his large and modern manufacturing facility. I went with them to Tabriz Grand Bazar where everyone was speaking in Turkish, and the guy who took me in a late-model BMW complained that all television shows were in Farsi and other ethnic tongues were totally ignored in schools and in the media. That was probably the reason that older ethnic Turks insisted on speaking Turkish—to preserve their mother tongue. He mentioned that young people in Azerbaijan felt their language was somewhat inferior and looked down at their parents who spoke only Turkish. It was the shah's policy to further unite the country by having everyone speak Farsi, by far the most dominant language. In doing so, however, he alienated people of many different languages and dialects in Iran. I always thought by teaching major ethnic languages like Turkish, Armenian, and Arabic in appropriate regions of the country along with Farsi, the country could have a much better connection with her neighbors while keeping Farsi as the official language shared by all Iranians.

We made a commercial for Lyco in London that included an attractive young lady in her nightgown covering her daughter with a Lyco comforter accompanied by the jingle, "Sweet dreams with Lyco!" in Farsi. After showing the commercial a few times on national television, the client showed up at our office and asked us to cut down the part of the mother and tone down the music since they had received many complaints about the woman in a nightgown. This was quite surprising to me since we had never had an issue before. As early as 1977, media was becoming quite conservative with respect to accepting advertising with the remotest connotation to sex or alcohol. In the past, we had women waterskiing in our Mum deodorant TV commercials, but the *Keyhan* paper with mostly

English-speaking readership had rejected our black-and-white Singapore Airlines advertisement for inflight service because the readers may have interpreted a glass with a dark shadow inside as wine!

Around that time, I was invited to represent the advertising industry in explaining the role of women in advertising in Iran during a primetime TV show with an audience of about 25 million throughout the country. Jaleh Kazemi, a popular Iranian television personality produced and hosted the show. At the time, NIRT was covering about 80 percent of the geographic area of Iran, which is about two-and-half times larger than the state of Texas. It covered all major cities and was by far the most dominant medium in Iran. In the studio after the introduction, a clip was played of a middle-aged man vehemently complaining about Western-style advertising, particularly the frequent presence of women in television commercials. In response, I mentioned that Iranian women were the main decision-makers and purchasers of a variety of items, especially toiletry products, cosmetics, home appliances, and countless other products and services; it was natural for many brands to connect with women. I gave the example of cosmetics advertising in which it would be strange to show a man wearing lipstick! Many friends and clients had seen the interview and were supportive of what I had to say but my comments didn't sit well with the most conservative and fanatic viewers who, according to Mr. Afshar from the NITR, were sending hate letters and condemning the participation of women in advertising.

After Alan moved from the Agency to the client side, I needed to hire an experienced account director from London. I asked Drummond Challis, my contact in London, to place an employment advertisement on our behalf and send me the applications. There was a pretty good response and we had several well- qualified candidates. I hired a person whom I thought was tough enough to handle the Iranian business environment. I met his lovely wife and daughter who visited him in Iran and were thinking of joining him in Tehran.

Unfortunately, our timing for hiring was awful; there were widespread demonstrations everywhere and only a short period of calm before the storm soon engulfed the entire country. The arrival of our new employee's furniture at customs coincided with the shah's departing Iran in January 1979 and the country's institutions were in the process of dismantling. Most of our international clients had left and there were no prospects for us to stay in business. I was concerned about the Englishman's safety and urged him to leave the country amid that chaotic situation. Most expatriates and their families as well as countless Iranians were trying to get out of the country. I knew there was little chance for our business to return to what it was in the short-term. I bought a hard-to-get airline ticket with the help of a friend who was running the Jordan Airlines local office to get our employee out of the country. It was one of lowest point in my life; losing my business' best assets—my employees and clients—who I had worked so hard to develop over the years!

Sitting from left: My mother holding my sister Fariba, my youngest brother Farhad, and my dad. Standing from left: My younger brother Farrokh and me in Tehran, Iran in 1955.

I am on the top right corner in this dormitory formal group photo, University of Maryland, 1965.

A wedding picture of Sherry and me, Tehran, Iran in 1973.

I am hosting a dinner for our client Bristol Myers at the Tehran Hilton Hotel around 1976. I am on the far left next to Mrs. Peterson. On her right is Firouz, the general manager next to his wife, On the far right is Eric Peterson, marketing manager, next to my wife Sherry.

From left: Willi Schalk, a BBDO vice president (standing), me, John Thompson, and from Impact-BBDO, Alain Khouri. BBDO, New York, 1977.

Sherry and Mike in Tehran, a few months before the Islamic Revolution and compulsory hijab in Tehran, Iran in 1978.

CHAPTER 4

Iran's Islamic Revolution

I was in my office around 6 p.m. on January 16, 1979, when I heard the unthinkable news. One of my employees told me anxiously that the shah left Iran and suggested that I take off my tie to blend in better as I went home. Later, I saw massive crowds on the streets and a young man holding up the front page of the evening newspaper with headlines in large letters saying, "The shah left!" There was much jubilation and excitement on the streets but I could hear gunfire and wasn't sure whether soldiers were fighting revolutionaries or the shots were part of the celebration. The Admen-BBDO office was in the Basiri building on the corner of the Villa and Shah Reza Avenues, a 45-minute drive from my house in the Farmanieh area. As I made a right turn, a teenager placed a poster of Ayatollah Khomeini's portrait under my right windshield wiper. I had no idea whether the poster was an asset in getting me through the streets or a liability if loyalist soldiers were ahead.

As I drove, a variety of thoughts entered my mind at the same time. I had always lived under the shah, a symbol of the country's pride, stability, and security. He fled Iran in 1953 but returned with the help of the US and the UK. However, this time it looked different; he had no visible supporters on the streets, the powerful armed forces of Iran were on the verge of collapse, and there was no indication that either the US or the UK could save him this time around. The enormity of what had just happened had huge implications for the future of my family, my business, and the country. As I headed to my neighborhood, I took a shortcut through an older area of Meehan Street that was narrow, a bit curvy, and passed by a mosque.

It was just getting dark as I approached the mosque, and I saw the silhouettes of a large crowd walking toward me. I immediately knew taking the shortcut was a mistake that day! I had to stop and soon the crowd of mostly young men surrounded my car. I was sure they had just listened to a fiery sermon about the shah's extravagances, corruption, and the oppression of the people; many angry faces who were probably looking for a target peered at me. Clean-shaven and wearing a Cecil Gee suit sitting in my luxury American car and living in the upscale Farmanieh area not too far away from the shah's palace, I hardly could fit the bill of a revolutionary.

I got the feeling they were poised to break my windows and attack me or possibly burn my car. As they gathered closer, I thought of Sherry and Mike ready for me to have dinner with them; I was petrified! I decided that sitting and waiting was not an option. I opened the driver's side door and stood on the running board of the large Buick Skylark so I was higher than all of them. In a strong voice, I told them the shah had just left and everyone was celebrating on the streets; the people were looking forward to welcoming Ayatollah Khomeini. As I spoke, I pointed to the poster of Khomeini that the teenager had left on my windshield. I knew this could go either way, but I felt the little speech and the poster saved the day as the crowd started to leave without uttering a word, although a few banged hard on my trunk as they walked away. I got home and found it quite difficult to explain to Sherry what I had just experienced.

About a year earlier in late December of 1977, President Jimmy Carter was the shah's guest and raised his champagne glass, honoring the shah and praising Iran as the "island of stability." Little did he know that in less than two years, the United States embassy in Tehran would be attacked and more than 50 of its embassy personnel taken hostage for 444 days. About a week after President Carter left Iran, *Ettela'at*, a major Farsi daily newspaper in Iran, published a derogatory article about Ayatollah Khomeini that resulted in a large protest in Qom, the second most significant religious city (after Mashhad) and one of the largest centers for Shia scholarship in the world. About three years earlier, a similar demonstration in Qom had been violently suppressed, but this time, demonstrations expanded to other cities and gradually turned into massive protest walks in Tehran and elsewhere.

The initial protest walks in Tehran were started at mosques by less privileged people who were primarily from south of Tehran and who had strong religious affiliations. They lived in dilapidated houses in crowed neighborhoods with heavy pollution. They had to cope with hyperinflation, a lack of health care, and poor nutrition. These people were unable to identify with Westernized fashions, cosmetic products, home appliances, and lifestyles regularly portrayed in entertainment, media, and advertising. I once spent time with a couple of these people when in the south of Tehran traveling in a Canda Dry truck to get a better sense of their distribution and their points of sales. We had breakfast together in a tea house where they served scrambled eggs in a large aluminum bowl with oven-fresh *sangak* bread. They were all eating with their hands from the same bowl and when they asked me to join them, I reluctantly accepted since I didn't want to offend them. They spoke freely and one man told me that he worked long hours but could hardly pay the rent for a small room in a house where he and his family were living; buying basic home appliances like a television set or even a refrigerator was out of question. They had no faith in the government or people wearing suits and ties and one mentioned that he knew a family with four children who were so poor that sometimes they only had bread with Canda Dry orange soda for lunch!

Another critical group that helped fuel the uprising in its early stages was agricultural workers who had left their families back in their villages and small towns and migrated to Tehran and other large cities to work in the booming construction industry due to the country's massive influx of oil revenues. A group of those migrants were living and working in an incomplete building close to our house. Every night they had bread, feta cheese, and green grapes—or melon in the summer. Until 9 or 10 p.m. they sang their folkloric village songs and used metal buckets as drums. Most people treated them as if they were invisible since they were not integrated into city life. NIRT portrayed them during popular shows as stupid characters like Samad with scruffy clothing and a village accent who was created and played by Parviz Sayyad. And there was the Ghooch Ali character who was extremely stupid and very overweight. In fact, the word "villager" in Farsi, *dahati*, was considered an insult. These people hardly benefited from the oil boom; the only place they were welcomed and felt comfortable was the mosque where they were encouraged to participate in religious mourning processions. In addition, food that was occasionally served in mosques during religious celebrations and mourning events was an attraction. They could easily identify with most clerics and Ayatollah Khomeni who had a provincial accent, but they could hardly understand and identify with the shah's eloquent speeches about his White Revolution and the promise of "great civilization" that seemed to target the middle class, foreign-educated, and elites of the country.

As protest walks gathered steam and thousands of people participated, the middle class and more affluent people gained enough confidence to joins the demonstrations to express their dissatisfaction with the government. I was beginning to share their frustrations as it seemed we were losing the race against time; it was taking months to clear imports from customs because of congestion in the major ports of Bandar Abbas on the Strait of Hormuz as well as Bandar Bushehr, Khorram-shahr, and Bandar Shahpur on the Persian Gulf, among other ports. The trucking industry and customs facilities were unable to handle the massive influx of goods from the West. Drug and alcohol use was rapidly rising, especially among the young or uneducated and there were many stories of domestic abuse that law enforcement and the courts were unable to handle. It was difficult for women to walk in public without being verbally harassed and occasionally sexually attacked by those who were not used to living in the city.

There were many first-time drivers on the roads and accidents and traffic jams were everywhere, plus, there was no insurance available. Many accident victims died because ambulances, hospital capacity, and health care personnel were in short supply. My brother Farrokh was a medical intern in Sina Hospital, the largest trauma center in Tehran, and told me a lot of accident patients were just thrown in a room overnight without any care.

It was clear that the country had no plan or the infrastructure to absorb the enormous newfound revenues as oil prices quadrupled. In the final analysis, the anger and frustration of all groups with a diverse set of issues and complaints crystalized into a message of hatred directed at the shah and his backers, especially the United States. Most people naively saw the solution to most of their problems was to remove the shah, whom they perceived to be standing between them and democracy. One of the main themes of the uprising was "the spring of freedom," but no one knew what it meant!

The scope and intensity of anti-shah demonstrations shocked the government. It was obvious that the Islamic and Marxist militants were turning the peaceful walks and demonstrations into violent confrontations with the police and the army. The government apparently had no idea how to contain the uprising. Unfortunately, instead of having an open discussion about the situation and seeking a national solution, the shah's regime was ignoring the entire situation and the government-controlled media was—ironically—reporting that all was under control. I saw a weather forecaster on television reporting the weather with hand gestures and tone of voice that told people nonverbally where in the country demonstrations were most intense!

On Friday, September 8, 1978, I was in Paris having a meeting with Steve Khaler from BBDO when I heard the word *Jaleh* and *Iran* repeatedly on the French radio but I had no idea what was going on. When I called people in Tehran, nobody knew anything about it either but later we learned that the police had opened fire on a large demonstration in Jaleh Square in Tehran, killing close to 100 people and injuring many more. The day, known in Iran as Black Friday, was on the heel of an incident when unknown assailants deliberately burned the movie theater Cinema Rex in Abadan southeast of Iran, and hundreds of people died behind the locked doors. By not being completely open and transparent about what was unfolding in the country, the media allowed news from foreigners and underground militant sources, as well as rumors and gossip to shape a negative and often false narrative against the government.

As the events were getting out of hand on Black Friday, the shah declared martial law in major cities and all street demonstrations were banned. One of the byproducts of martial law was that most of our clients who were incommunicado showed up and willingly paid all their bills in cash, as opposed to the ordinary six-month promissory notes because they were afraid of facing military tribunals and being charged with collaborating with the revolutionaries. In response to the widespread demonstrations and strikes, the shah went through several heads of cabinets in a short time after he fired his long-time prime minister, Abbas Hoveyda, who was later executed by the Islamic regime. Even martial law could not pacify the country.

In response to the chaotic situation, the shah named General Azhari, an army officer, as the interim prime minister, who immediately ordered a dusk-to-dawn curfew. Every police station became like a fortress as policemen stood outside it with automatic weapons. Additionally, Imperial Guardsmen camped near the shah's palace on the street close to our house. According to the tradition in Iran, people hold memorials on the seventh and 40th day of the anniversary of the deceased. So, the Jaleh Square Massacre (Black Friday) perpetuated the force of demonstrations as more people were killed during numerous protests at memorial events. Night after night, passionate anti-shah sermons delivered in mosques later translated into massive demonstrations in defiance of the curfew. Every night, there was a blackout disrupting people's lives and pushing the scene of protests to the rooftops where they chanted "God is great!" in many neighborhoods in solidarity with the revolutionaries. Around the same period, there was a rumor that Ayatollah Khomeini's portrait was going to appear on the full moon. Of course, if one looked hard enough, it was possible to imagine a portrait with a turban out of the dark shadows on the moon. The next day, a couple of people, including our maid, said they saw Khomeini's portrait on the full moon.

During the curfew period, Mike, just three-and-a-half years old, was running a high fever and we had to take him to the hospital. Unfortunately, the curfew was already in effect and soldiers were authorized to shoot violators. We were told the curfew would end at 4 a.m., so Sherry and I kept putting cold towels on Mike's forehead, washing his feet with cold water, and giving him some cold medicine but he was still burning hot. That was one of the longest nights of my life. Shortly after 4 a.m., I started driving toward Tajrish Square Hospital while Sherry held Mike in her arms. The streets were eerily quiet and after driving about a quarter of a mile, I heard someone yelling in the dark telling us to stop. When I did, I saw a soldier on each side of my car lying on their stomachs aiming their long guns at us. A third soldier approached the window with a gun in his hand—we were so frightened to have three guns aimed at us! We explained our situation and he told us the curfew would end at 5 a.m., but fortunately they let us continue to the hospital where they took care of Mike.

In October of 1978, I went to New York for a meeting at BBDO. I flew with Iran Air, the fastest growing airline in the world at the time. Many of the passengers were young, religious, and supported the Islamic uprising. After I had a gin and tonic, a guy sitting next to me who was part of a large group admonished me about drinking alcohol. He was following the Islamic principal of "promoting virtue and preventing vice." During his conversation with his friend, I gathered that his father was a Shia cleric; it seemed the clerics were sending their children to Europe and America for safety during the uprising even as they attacked the decadent lifestyles of the West.

During my stay in New York, I met Alain Khouri from Impact-BBDO who was also participating in the meetings. I had felt sorry for him because of the civil war and violence in Lebanon during the 1970s; little did I know that I was about to meet the same fate. I had a feeling that Iran was rapidly losing its prestige and image in the world—an image that the shah had crafted over the years, distinguishing Iran from other countries in the region by capitalizing on his multilingual skills and Western education and intimate familiarity with its culture. He was indeed a great imagemaker for Iran, unlike Shia clerics with turbans and beards who promoted black hijabs for all women.

When I returned from the US, there were widespread labor strikes in support of the uprising, including the critical oil sector. Without oil revenue, the collapse of any regime in Iran is a certainty! In November and December of 1978, gasoline was in great shortage. Once I was in a gasoline line for about 30 hours so I left my gas guzzling Buick Skylark there in line overnight and got a ride home. During other long waits in the car, I read two complete books, *Working*, a 1974 book by Studs Terkel exploring the meaning of work for different people and different circumstances, and *Roots: The Saga of an American Family*, a 1976 book by Alex Haley. It was a novel but real for many people who were stolen from their families and sold in slave markets in the US. It was hard to fathom the degree of savagery and heartlessness and I felt so sad about the horrible plight of the enslaved Africans. Later, I learned that slaves originally were white and the slave trade had been going on long before America was discovered.

One of the significant aspects of Shia militancy is the sense of injustice and martyrdom amplified in its culture and embedded in one of its significant historical events: the martyrdom of Imam Hussein, a Shia hero and role model for Shia warriors. Imam Hussein was the son of Imam Ali, the prophet's son-in-law, who was, according to Shia Muslims, the first caliph (Muhammad successor) of Islam, followed by 11 others according to the blood line. The Sunnis, however, believe that the Prophet's successors were Abubakr, Umar, and Uthman who were successively elected by consensus and Ali succeeded them as the fourth caliph. Hossein, the third imam of Shia Muslims, sought to overthrow the powerful Umayyad Caliph Yazid to become the rightful caliph of Islam. In an epic battle near Karbala, a city in current Iraq, during the 10th day of Muharram, the first Islamic lunar month, in 680 AD, Imam Hossein, his two sons, and his loyal warriors faced a much larger army and were all tragically killed by the Umayyad caliph, Yazid. While the elaborate mourning rituals for Karbala's event were banned during Reza Shah's reign, the current shah allowed them.

Every Muharram as I was growing up, the country mourned the martyrdom of Imam Hossein. The sermons and singing of *nohe*, or mourning poems, praising the bravery of Hossein and the injustices of Yazid was everywhere including the media and mosques' loudspeakers. Temporary mosques, called *Husseinieh* or *Takieh*, were set up for people to mourn the death of Imam Hussein about a thousand years earlier. There was also a reenactment of the Karbala battle across the country. Our neighbor Haji Mofid opened his large house during the month of Muharram for commemorating the Karbala battle events. The men and women were separated by a curtain and you could hear the loud cry of women mourning Hussein's martyrdom. Some of the clergy were good at singing *nohe*; Mr. Zabihi, a popular clergyman, had a particularly great voice and was often heard on the radio. It was hard to tell whether he was singing a song or prayers; unfortunately, he was killed by the Islamic revolutionaries in 1979 for cooperating with the shah's regime.

In 1954, my parents and our extended family spent a summer in a garden house in Fasham to escape Muharram's mourning ceremonies and the brutal heat of Tehran. I loved the cooler weather, fruit gardens, rivers, and hills of Fasham, a mountainous village about 20 miles north of Tehran. I was nine years old and had so much fun hiking with my older cousins and aunts on a hill right behind the garden house and swimming in the nearby rivers.

One afternoon in Fasham, I saw a show called *Tazieh*, a reenactment of the martyrdom of Imam Hussein. The show focused on how bravely Hussein, his brother, Abbas, and his

147

valiant warriors fought a much larger army. The performance was in the center of the village on a dirt stage with hundreds of villagers watching. They also reenacted the barbaric treatment of women and children and their great suffering and humiliation after the death of Imam Hussein. It was a two-hour show with a script and costumes occasionally accompanied with singing of mourning poetry. Women in the audience were crying out loud, and I witnessed the sorrow and anger in the faces of the villagers. Karbala reenactments were shown in every village and town on the Day of Ashura when it all happened. I had seen men and women cry publicly as clergies described the Karbala events during the month of Muharram and on other occasions.

Large processions, mainly in the south of Tehran and provinces, were strictly for men. Some carried flags and *alam*, a large heavy metal covered with symbolic metal figures, borne by an athletic man. Men wore black shirts with openings on the front and two openings on the backs for beating their chests or hitting their upper backs with small chains in time with cymbals accompanied by chanting or singing of mourning poems. In the south of Tehran and other poor neighborhoods, true believers put mud on their heads and hit their foreheads softly with a blade. The exact day of the event is called *ashura*, the 10th of Moharram, when major processions take place. Injustice and martyrdom are prominent themes in Shia literature and culture.

These themes were in full bloom at the University of Tehran, the hotbed of political protests during the uprising in 1978 and where I saw a spectrum of groups and ideologies promoting different causes. Most had tables and were selling

148

books, audio cassettes, pamphlets, and posters advancing their vision of Iran, ranging from an Islamic government to Western liberal democracy to socialism and even communism. Each promised justice and freedom for all! I also saw posters of some of the champions of these causes who had been executed by the shah's regime, such as Khosrow Gole Sorkhi, a journalist, poet, and, allegedly, a communist. The audio cassette equipment, some of which I had helped import from TDK for music when I was in Japan, was being used for duplication and distribution of the fiery speeches of Ayatollah Khomeini and others. I saw many books and cassette tapes from a popular icon of the revolution, Ali Shariati, who had a PhD in sociology from the University of Paris and was the son of a cleric who had passed about a year earlier. Ali Shariati's writings and speeches glorified Islam by showcasing the Islamic contributions to the sciences and humanities, especially in the Middle Ages in contrast to Europe during that period. His pro-democracy ideas had broad appeal among the young and the middle class and attracted many educated people to Shia Islam, but they were mostly ignored by the extreme and ultraconservative Shia clerics who took over the revolution.

In the 1970s, the country saw the mass production of wine for the first time under the *Pakdis* brand. During the uprising, growers in Azerbaijan were pressured by the clerics not to supply grapes to the company since production and consumption of alcoholic beverages is strictly forbidden in Islam although wine was part of the Iranian culture for many centuries as indicated by the historical documents, poetry, and ancient artifacts. The production manager, an older Swiss man, was living close to my house in Farmanieh. When he called me, I was quite surprised that he was still around since I heard his boss, Vahabzadeh, had fled the country.

The Swiss invited me to a meeting and told me that Vahabzadeh had just returned from an atonement trip from *Imam Hussein* shrine in Karbala, Iraq, asking forgiveness for making wine and vodka. He told me they were getting out of the business of making alcoholic beverages and it was very important that I went to the meeting. The next day, I met with Vahabzadeh, a major businessman and owner of the Pakdis brand, in the BMW building on Roosevelt Ave. that he owned. Vahabzadeh told me he was going to mass produce a new type of juice under the brand Sundiz and package it in some type of laminate layer with a straw that was quite innovative at the time. This non-alcoholic drink was going to compete with other soft drinks like Coca-Cola and Pepsi. He wanted to see creative and media plans for a budget of about a $1 million to launch Sundiz as soon as possible. I was so happy when I left the meeting; this was a much needed shot in the arm for the stagnating business, providing a bright spot in a gloomy environment of uprising.

On my way to work the next day, I went to pass by the BMW building where we had our meeting the day before, but it wasn't there! To be sure, I made a U-turn at the end of the street and was absolutely flabbergasted to see a major branch of Bank-e-Melli was burned down to the ground and furniture and papers scattered on the street. Unfortunately, the BMW building was also completely burned. This was the scene in every part of northern Tehran that day—piles of furniture and junk on the streets burning. Sherry told me that from her office, she saw paperwork being thrown from the windows of a high-rise building like confetti, not to mention the furniture thrown in the middle of the street. This was a coordinated campaign of terror organized by the Islamic Marxists to deliver a fatal blow to the shah's regime.

Toward the end of 1978, the shah made a final effort by giving a passionate speech telling the Iranians that he had heard their voice and would try to respond to their legitimate demands. On December 29, 1978, he appointed Shapour Bakhtiar , a long-time critic of his policies and one of the leaders of the National Front, a pro-democracy organization founded by Dr. Mossadegh who nationalized the Iranian oil industry.

The shah left Iran in early January 1979, and on February 1, Ayatollah Khomeini arrived in Tehran in a chartered Air France Boeing 747 together with his large entourage and quite a few journalists, and that day became a national holiday in Iran. Khomeini had been staying in Neauphle-le-Chateau, France after Saddam Hossein deported him from Iraq in October of 1978. Khomeini received initial worldwide visibility and name recognition while in France, thanks to the French and international media. On television, I saw Khomeini onboard the chartered Air France flight to Tehran when a reporter asked him what he felt to be returning to Iran after living in exile for 14 years. His answer was a shocking, "nothing!" Later, it became clear to me that Khomeini had a grand vison of creating a nation of Islam in the Middle East, beyond the borders of Iran—a goal that has been pursued by the Islamic Republic of Iran since its inception at all costs. When his plane landed in Mehrabad International Airport, the Air France pilot helped him down the airstairs with a group of clerics following him.

Like millions of people, Sherry and I were curious and wanted to see him as he was going straight from the airport to

Tehran's main cemetery, Behesht-e-Zahra, to pay respects to those who had died during the uprising. Millions of people on his route were standing on top of cars and buildings and sitting on tree branches. Khomeini's motorcade arrived after an hour or so, moving slowly. It was the most chaotic scene; hundreds of people, mostly armed, were hanging from vans, trucks, and buses and many covered Khomeini's van with their bodies on the front, sides, and top. We could hardly see him. He was just waving his hand slowly with no other sign of greeting. Khomeini made a speech at Behesht-e-Zahra cemetery, which I later saw on television. He said something to the effect that people should not expect a quick fix for all the damage that the shah had inflicted on Iran and that the shah had emptied the treasury and filled cemeteries. Khomeini was a great communicator who could influence the masses with his grandfatherly and provincial accent, repeating simple words and phrases as opposed to the shah whose speech was strictly for the educated Iranians and the population of Europe and America.

I never heard Khomeini distinguishing between Shia and Sunni, but I felt he was planning to make Iran a powerbase of exporting the revolution to other Islamic nations, especially those with a considerable Shia population. First, needed to win the hearts and minds of a broad group of educated Iranians with diverse backgrounds, especially younger people. In doing so, he initially surrounded himself with a group of non-clerics, moderate, pro-democracy activists and politicians who were relatively young, educated, and had some pro-democracy credentials. As part of his entourage, Khomeini brought with him to Tehran three non-clerical individuals with long records of pro-democracy and anti-shah activism in Europe and America. The trio, in turn, was hoping to use Khomeini to bring democracy to Iran; Abolhassan Bani Sadr was promoting the Islamic government from a democratic perspective among the university and intellectual types and became the first president of the Islamic Republic of Iran. In 1981, his liberal interpretation of Islam drastically clashed with the extremely conservative clerics who were gaining power in Iran and he was impeached and went into hiding. He managed to escape from Iran to France together with Rajavi, the head of the People's Mujahedin, with the help of his pilot, Behzad Moezi. Bani Sadr was granted political asylum in France under the condition that he would refrain from conducting any political activities in France. I met Colonel Moezi in Seattle in the early 1980s at the home of a friend and neighbor in Bellevue, Washington. Colonel Moezi described his heroic escape out of Iran flying President Bani Sadr on an Iranian Air Force Boeing 707.

Another person who arrived with Khomeini was Ebrahim Yazdi, a pharmacist who had lived in the United States and, after the revolution, was promoting the Islamic movement among military personnel. When we visited Sherry's brother Mike in Houston, Texas, where Yazdi had been living, some friends told us that they had seen a remarkable difference in Yazdi's family finances—including their furniture, dishes, and jewelry after he accompanied Khomeini to Iran. Yazdi became a deputy prime minister and minister of foreign affairs during the first interim cabinet after the revolution headed by Mehdi Bazargan, who was also a liberal democrat. Like Bazargan, Yazdi resigned in protest of the government-sanctioned invasion of the US embassy and taking personnel hostage. He was arrested several times and died in Turkey in 2017.

The third non-cleric person with Khomeini was Sadegh Ghotbzadeh, who took over the Iranian National Radio and Television and became the minister of foreign affairs during the hostage crisis. His ideas also clashed with the ultraconservative clerics and he was politically isolated. Later, he was convicted of criticizing the Islamic Republic and conspiring with Tudeh Communist Party's army officers to blow up Khomeini's house and kill the entire regime's leadership. In 1982, he made a televised confession and was executed shortly after in Evin Prison.

February 4–11, 1979, Iran had two competing prime ministers: the shah's Shapour Bakhtiar and Khomeini's Mehdi Bazargan. Both the shah and Khomeini knew the Iranian people wanted freedom and democracy, so both appointed French-educated and pro-democracy individuals who had worked with Mossadegh, a pro-democracy icon who had stood up against the West and nationalized the Iranian oil industry in the early 1950s. The shah still had his Imperial Armed Forces intact, and Khomeni had the passionate support of people on the streets. Based on media reports, President Carter, like his predecessors, was worried that Iran's vast oil, gas, and natural resources may fall in the hands of the Soviet Union, not to mention losing a significant geostrategic ally and partner. Carter sent General Robert E. Huyser to Iran in early January 1979 to explore US options in Iran and organize a coup in favor of Bakhtiar or, alternatively, ensure the Iranian military would not prevent the creation of an Islamic regime as opposed to a pro-Soviet Marxist regime.

A family member who was a high-ranking military officers told me General Fardoust, the powerful head of the Imperial Inspectorate and the childhood friend of the shah, was encouraging senior generals, most of whom were his protégés, not to crack down on demonstrators who were becoming a larger group and more radical. The inaction probably contributed to the shah's gradual loss of his grip on power, leading to Carter's decision of supporting Khomeini. I heard General Fardoust was instrumental in encouraging General Gharabaghi, the chief of staff of the Imperial Armed Forces of Iran, to tell Bakhtiar that the armed forces would remain neutral in the fight between the shah's regime and Khomeini followers. His stance caused the dismantling of Iran's military and the collapse of the Bakhtiar government, paving the way for the eventual creation of the Islamic Republic of Iran.

The same source told me that General Fardoust took refuge in the home of General Mohammad Gharani the first night after the collapse of the shah's regime. Gharani served as the first chief of staff of the Iranian Army after the Iranian Revolution and was later assassinated.

We witnessed the total collapse of the Imperial Armed Forces of Iran, one of the strongest in the region. My brother-in-law was doing his military service when he was told to go home; he came home with a couple of automatic weapons and handguns, but his father made him get rid of them. Military bases were looted and the police station close to our house was ransacked. I saw young boys of around 12 and 13 carrying long guns and police helmets from the police station, which had looked like a fortress just a couple of weeks before. The armed youth roamed around town. When Sherry and I were on our way to visit her parents, a group of armed teenagers driving what looked like a parent's BMW stopped us and checked my trunk for weapons. We saw the neighborhood vegetable man carrying a long gun as though he was on a mission. I asked him where he was heading; he told me he was going to kill his mother-in-law. He looked serious!

The Shia clerics quickly took control and dominated the other groups. They were ready—they had a charismatic leader in Ayatollah Khomeini and his doctrine of *Valayat Fagheeh* (guardianship of the Islamic jurist), the tradition of Shia Islam in Iran and the strong network of mosques and clerics with superb persuasive and oratory skills, along with the US administration's support of the Islamic regime that they thought could block communist aggression in Iran. Islamic committees were quickly set up in every mosque and acted as police, jury, and judge. Arabic and Koranic phrases were abundant and terms floated about like "corruptor of earth" which carried a death penalty and was reserved for top-level military officers and the most senior-level civil servants who were brought in front of the Revolutionary Court.

During the following days, I saw many blindfolded people taken away to unknown locations. Ayatollah Khomeini used Rafah Elementary, a girls' school in the Sarcheshemeh area in Tehran, as his temporary headquarters. He gave speeches from the balcony of the school in the area where my maternal great grandparents had lived years earlier. People behind a curtain would remind him from time to time if he was missing anything in his speeches; it was normally about thanking a special group that he had neglected to mention.

Every night, the evening papers prominently displayed pictures of the dead bodies of famous military and government officials who were convicted and executed on the roof of the school with automatic weapons by the Revolutionary Court. Some of the so-called trials were also shown on television. Out of curiosity, my father-in-law and I went to the school to see what was going on. There, I saw some of my former students at the Imperial Air Force Language School among hundreds of non-commissioned officers called *Homafar* who were blocking the school building with their sheer numbers.

During the first days of the Islamic regime, some restaurants were still serving wine and vodka pretending they were coke and water. But things were getting tighter as the Islamic government took more control. Committees formed in mosques around the country were enforcing the Islamic rules as ordered by the clergy in charge of that mosque who, in turn, was taking orders from Khomeini and his aides. Women without a hijab were harassed on the streets. The committees were invading people's homes and, if they suspected a party or if they found any alcoholic beverages, they would arrest and flog everyone in the house, their punishment of choice. They invaded the homes of a relative to take all my wife's cousins for flogging. Some jumped from a second-floor balcony into the pool out of fear and injured themselves. My brother-in-law, Saeed, who became Simon, showed me the imprint of the many lashes he received on his back.

Right after the collapse of the shah's regime, I saw quite a few Palestinian men driving around in Tehran with their special *Kufiyyeh* scarves in military jeeps that had been abandoned by the shah's armed forces. The first foreign leader to visit Iran after the Islamic Revolution was Yasser Arafat, the leader of the Palestinian Liberation Organization (PLO); I saw him with Khomeini's son, Ahmad, on television. Revolutionary songs in support of the Palestinian freedom and the annihilation of Israel were constantly played on the radio and television. The Israel embassy was turned into the PLO office in Tehran, and the daily chant of "death to Israel" became a ritual in most private and formal gatherings. The Arab governments had practically abandoned the Palestinian cause by either making peace with Israel or avoiding a war with it. In contrast, the Islamic regime embraced the Palestinian cause, providing religious and political justification for their choice. The religious justification was based on one of the most important tenets of Shia Islam, namely justice. Revolutionaries often demonstrated for the plight of Palestinian people who, according to them, were oppressed by Israel and the United States. The revolutionaries positioned themselves as defenders of the oppressed around the world, including Palestinians. This thinking created a body of language and institutions in Iran. For example, the huge Pahlavi Foundation was renamed to Mostazafan Foundation, or the Foundation of the Oppressed People. In my view, the strategic political aspect of the Palestinian cause was to inflame anti-Israeli and anti-American passions in the Arab population to create tension and, ultimately, destabilize Arab countries thus paving the way for engineering an Iranian-style revolution in those countries.

As to the causes of the Iranian Revolution, well, Iranians love conspiracy theories. With respect to the fall of the Pahlavi Regime, several conspiracy theories have been floating among the Iranian people for decades: some suggest that the US had a long-term plan to remove the shah because he was becoming too powerful and was refusing to sign a new oil contract with the West; the shah had suggested the price of oil be connected to the price of a basket of Western products to safeguard oil revenues against imported inflation. Others point to the US desire to replace the monarchy with an Islamic regime in Iran to block the expansion of the communist Soviets in the Middle East since in the neighboring Afghanistan, the pro-America Islamic rebels known as Mujahideen were fighting the Soviet-backed Democratic Government of Republic of Afghanistan. Mr. Zbigniew Brzezinski, President Carter's national security advisor, was in Pakistan telling the Mujahedeen to redouble their efforts against infidels and get back their county and their mosques.

It is not unreasonable to think that the United States and Europe did not want to let the Soviet Union control the vast oil and gas resources of Iran or take over a valuable geostrategic part of the world, including access to the Persian Gulf and beyond. Based on that assumption, we may attribute the destabilization of the shah's regime and its eventual fall to the Soviet's propaganda and terroristic actions inside Iran by its affiliated Marxist and militant clerical groups. Some argue that the shah focused on the Marxists and was oblivious to the underground activities of ultraconservative militant clerics. In the final analysis, the establishment of the Islamic Republic may be a combination of those factors, since no one knows with absolute certainty. We can safely say that Russia emerged as the main beneficiary of the creation of the Islamic Republic of Iran.

Right after the establishment of the provisional government early in 1979, a meeting was scheduled for all advertising-related businesses at the offices of Pakhshiran Company, the major organization for placement of commercials in the movie theaters around the country. The meeting, held in a large screening room, was to discuss the fate of our industry and to elect new syndicate board members since some of the old board members had fled the country. I was elected to the board along with Ahmad Abdoli, my former boss at Caspian Advertising, Inc., and several others. The names of new board members were published that evening in either *Kayhan* or *Ettelaat*, major national newspapers. The mandate of the board was to negotiate a financial settlement with the media on behalf of the advertising syndicate and lobby the regime for the survival of the advertising industry. It turned out that the financial situation in the media was quite fluid and uncertain. Most media outlets were operating under the guidance of Islamic committees and their financial operations were dysfunctional. Young revolutionaries from Bazar were put in charge of advertising revenues while the whole industry was at a standstill. The younger Massoudi was my next-door neighbor and who ran the famous *Ettelaat* newspaper after his brother Farhad left the county. We witnessed revolutionaries invade his house and loot all his furniture; I never saw Massoud again and am hoping he managed to get out of the country with his family.

During the first week of the provisional government, I received a letter from a former business associate, Mr. Abraviz, who invited me to join a consultation meeting in the Kennedy Circle Mosque. Several of our syndicate board members were already there. Soon, the host appeared armed with a Colt handgun and a letter indicating that he was a member of the Islamic Republic Army. He talked for a few minutes about the need for equality in wealth and things of that nature; nobody took him seriously and we all got up and left.

Following that incident, we were summoned back to the mosque in Kennedy Circle to explain what had transpired. This time, a clergyman directed us into a room where Ayatollah Mohammad Beheshti and Ayatollah Mohammad Bahonar, who were among the founding members of the Islamic Republic

Party, were there. There were only about a dozen other people in the room. As we each entered the room, Ayatollah Beheshti stood up halfway as a sign of respect and humility. I had no idea that he was the second person in the political hierarchy of Iran and was the architect of the post-revolutionary constitution as well as the administrative structure of the Islamic Republic. After welcoming our small group, Beheshti said that he had lived in Germany for many years and was familiar with the Western advertising machine and referred to us as a small wave of that. He said he should soon rent a place for the Islamic Republic Party totally independent of the government. Bahonar went over a list from his old-fashioned Samsonite briefcase. The clergy in charge of Kennedy Circle Mosque was asked to explain Mr. Abraviz's activities in the mosque. The clergy said that he brought many different groups to the mosque including the architects, film-makers, and the advertising folks, and on each occasion, the groups had left after a short time. He said Abraviz liked to brandish his gun and they had attempted to confiscate it a couple of times, but Ayatollah Hashemi Rafsanjani, from the 25th of Shahrivar's committee, had told them to return his gun to him. A decade later, Rafsanjani became the president of Iran. About two years after I left Iran, Bahonar became the prime minister of Bani Sadr's government. People's Mujahedeen, a designated terrorist group by the US, assassinated Beheshti, Bahonar, and many others when I was in the United States.

As part of the advertising syndicate board, we met with a few other important people of the time. We visited the office of Ayatollah Taleghani, who had been recently freed from the notorious Evin Prison by the revolutionaries. I heard him ask why the shah's regime was always after the Russian spies and never arrested an American spy. We visited his home and met a man wearing a camouflage army jacket sitting behind a desk with a walkie-talkie in his hand and a deep scar on his forehead. He was complaining about several unauthorized committees confiscating people's assets in the name of Ayatollah Taleghani but who were not sharing their gains with them. It seemed he wanted to collect royalties from these other Islamic committees using the Ayatollah's name! In the meantime, while we were sitting in front of him, he was happily telling us that his people were confiscating the content of a warehouse that belonged to Hojabr Yazdani, a formerly prominent businessman, who had escaped to Costa Rica. One of our relatives who had attended the Islamic Alavi religious high school in Tehran before the revolution told me that right after the revolution, Mr. Yazdi invited the former students of Alavi, a religious high school, to supervise the businesses and properties confiscated by the Islamic revolutionaries, including those of Hojabr Yazdani. We also met with the minister of information, Nasser Minachi, a moderate figure from the days of the National Front. His office was extremely unorganized and additional chairs had to be brought into in a small room. I was the youngest member of the board, clean-shaven, and wore a nice suit and tie; he kept looking at my suit and tie and asking if our group had completely purged their ranks. Most of the formerly well-dressed and clean-shaven board members had grown beards and were wearing old jackets with no ties to better fit the new environment.

Soon, women were required to wear a hijab in the government buildings. Campaigns exalting the virtue of Islamic hijab hung posters in grocery shop windows and other high-traffic areas. In a last-ditch effort against the compulsory hijab, more than a thousand brave Iranian women in colorful outfits and makeup marched against the new rules on Shah Reza Avenue, passing by our offices. Men and women ridiculed the protesters and threw things at them. That day, we had to close our offices and say goodbye to smart, hardworking and loyal people with whom we had worked for years; it was one of the saddest days of my life! We gathered most of them and explained our situation, gave everyone one month of salary, and promised to hire them back as soon as we started working again. We kept one employee for the transition and closed the place. We all faced an uncertain future,

In late March of 1979, the provisional government of Iran organized a national referendum asking the Iranian people whether they agreed with the change of the country's name from "Imperial State of Iran" to "Islamic Republic of Iran." Everyone had to vote and get his or her birth certificate stamped. Mosques around the country became the polling stations, among other places. I went to vote at the mosque close to our house on Meehan Street, near where I had faced a mob coming out of the same mosque. The mosque looked like a fortress and young men wearing combat uniforms and full beards were behind sandbags. I entered a room where a group of clerics and some civilians were sitting on chairs next to the walls around the room; some held rosaries and seemed to be counting prayers. I signed in and received a piece of heavy paper perforated in the middle dividing the sheet in two parts: one part green and the other light yellow. The question was the same on both parts, asking whether I agreed with the name change and a new constitution that would put to a vote later.

The word YES in Farsi was written in the bottom of the green part and NO was written on the bottom of the yellow part. I was directed to a makeshift kiosk where I could detach the two parts and drop one in a box there. But the process was not as private as it may have seemed; once I deposited one part in the ballot box, I had to drop the other in an empty waste basket that was somewhat visible from the room and they could easily figure out my vote! I got my birth certificate signed and left. The change was approved by the voters and, when I was no longer in Iran, in December of 1979, people voted to replace the Iranian Constitution of 1906 with the Islamic Republic of Iran Constitution.

The idea of government-sponsored religion, however, did not sit well with me. I was awake most nights thinking about how to navigate my life through the revolution. I knew my decision would impact my life and Sherry's and, most important, that of Mike. I had a feeling that we were thrown into the seventh century. I often thought of leaving Iran for good, but that would create more uncertainty for us. Leaving Iran was not an easy decision since we had to leave our parents behind, with whom we were so close. They were also attached to Mike, especially Mr. Tavassoli, Sherry's dad. There was a sliver of hope that things would go back to normal. We were not sure how much money we needed and what we could do to survive in the US given my previous experience in America.

When the provisional government finally opened the borders after a few months in May 1979, I received a phone call from John Thompson inviting me to New York on behalf of BBDO, Inc. *Advertising Age*, a major publication for advertising and marketing in the US, was going to interview me about the future of advertising in Iran. I accepted and decided to take Sherry and Mike with me. I was thinking we could explore the idea of moving to the United States, albeit it seemed like a very long shot. Sherry had never been to the United States and I wanted her to see the country. Surprisingly sending money abroad was still possible, albeit with a 15-percent rate increase, so I sent some money to the US. Sherry agreed to come, and we decided to visit friends and family members in New York, Houston, Los Angeles, and Portland after my BBDO meeting. We both had multiple business entry visas and had to submit our passports five days prior to the travel date to get an exit permit from the new government. One of my friends advised me to write "self-employed" for the occupation question since they would deny exit visas to managing directors unless they got special clearance.

During our flight, I saw the man I had seen in Ayatollah Taleghani's office with a large black Samsonite, but instead of his camouflage combat uniform and beard, he had shaved and wore a clean European jacket. There was no way that I could be wrong, especially with the knife scar on his forehead. He got off in London. Later, when we were living in Seattle, Washington, I talked about him with Colonel Tayabi who had been the second in command of the police intelligence in Tehran during the shah's time. He knew the man and told me he was serving a long prison sentence for murder but was freed by the revolutionaries.

I wanted to talk about the importance of advertising in Iran during my interview but was not sure about the attitude of the new government toward it. I asked my maternal uncle Dr. Mohsen Moayedi, a professor at Farrah University who spoke Arabic and French, whether he knew anything about Islam's support of advertising. He quickly cited a verse from the holy book in which the prophet was told something like to go and advertise the religion. I took a note of that; I think that was the last time I saw him. He was critical of the shah's dictatorial policies, especially when he dissolved all the political parties in Iran. After the revolution, he was appointed as the president of Farah University based on student's votes, but after a month or so, the conservative clerics realized he was for liberal democracy and was not a supporter of a dictatorial clerical Shia regime; needless to say, was soon fired. When the *Advertising Age* reporter in New York asked me about the future of advertising in Iran, I was ready. I told her the future of advertising in Iran was good since the revolutionaries used advertising techniques such as handbills, wall posters, as well as recorded cassettes and jingles to communicate their messages. Even in the Islam holy book, the prophet was commanded to advertise the religion. They published the piece with my picture in the May 28, 1979, issue.

Most Iranians in the United States were in shock as their country's status had changed from a friendly ally of the United States to an enemy. They were uncertain about their future or whether they needed to return to Iran. One of our friends was the commandant of the Iranian Navy cadets studying in the US, and suddenly had his US visa revoked and the situation of the cadets was in a limbo. We visited Sherry's brother, Mike, and his family in Houston, Texas, who was in the process of building a restaurant and a skating rink—something that he had never done before. We also went to California, where my brother, Farrokh, had just completed his residency in radiology at Loma Linda Hospital. He was making plans to take his family back to Iran; he already had sent back his books and some light items. I suggested he should wait for a while since things were not settled in Iran and thankfully, he agreed.

In Loma Linda, Sherry and I were looking forward to having a drink and relaxing a bit after the long ordeal of living through a revolution. But we were both quite surprised to see how quiet the city was on a Friday night! That contrast with my perception of California as a vibrant place. My brother explained that most of the population were Seventh Day Adventists and they observed the sabbath from Friday evening to Saturday evening. In addition, what I had thought was meat in the supermarket earlier that day was actually plant-based meat since most of the population were strict vegetarians. I had heard that the Seventh Day Adventists lived a long life, now I knew what a reason might be. Farrokh got a temporary job at the military base in South Carolina; as an Iranian, he had to keep a low profile in a military environment in the face of the constant anti-American rhetoric coming from Iran.

We visited my old friend, Ali who ran the Cinegraphic Studio back in Tehran and with whom I used to create television commercials. He was in the process of creating a one-hour weekly Farsi TV program in the Los Angeles area. On the last leg of our trip, we went to Portland, Oregon, where Sherry's uncle, Fetullah, was living. He had been a successful businessman in Iran, but now, he had an antique rug shop in Portland. I loved the summer weather of Oregon; it was so mild, peaceful, and calming after a noisy and violent revolution. I bought a house on Wilderness Drive in West Linn, Oregon, as an investment and in case we had to leave Iran. It was a beautiful four-bedroom house with a large and gorgeous backyard without walls or fences.

We returned to a chaotic Iran; I was leaning toward leaving the country but still had not completely made up my mind about immigrating to the US. It looked like we needed a lot more money there than we had. Many of my friends and colleagues were leaving. The provisional government was in the process of collecting looted guns. Again, I was faced with a lot of difficult choices. One day I took Mike to Shahan Shahi Park, as I aways did, but it was the first time since the revolution There had been display cages for pheasants, parrots, and other birds but now, all the cages were empty since the birds had been released. Mike wanted to sit around the duck pond and watch the ducks. There, a teenage boy was hitting the ducks with slingshots, making Mike a bit anxious. I complained to a person with heavy beard who seemed to be in charge there, but he rudely said, "Iran sacrificed many lives in the revolution, and now you are worried about the ducks?" I heard that type of response many times after the revolution. Believe it or not, that was the straw that broke the camel's back. That night, I decided I didn't want to live in revolutionary Iran and that going to America was well worth all the risks that it involved.

CHAPTER 5

The Start of an Iranian Exodus

One early Saturday morning in August 1979, my Boeing 747 was taking off from Tehran Mehrabad International Airport; I was fleeing a totalitarian theocracy while embracing an uncertain life with the hope of a better future—just like most of the passengers on the crowded flight. Once again, I was leaving behind my family, friends, favorite places, and everything that I had worked for during the past 10 years! The provisional revolutionary government was tightening travel restrictions for more categories of people, including those who were senior government employees and private sector managing directors prior to the revolution. There was also a distrust of people with strong connections to the West, which would have included me as the managing director of Admen-BBDO with large American clients such as Colgate Palmolive, Bristol Myers, and Exxon. I was especially concerned about the interview with popular female journalist Jaleh Kazemi that I had given just before the start of the revolution on the NIRT. I had supported the use of female models in advertising by suggesting that we could not have a male model wearing lipstick to promote it. I had made that comment without thinking that there would soon be an ultra-Shia revolutionary government in Iran that might ban showing women's hair or even make it illegal for women to appear in television commercials. In addition, some of my associates had become self-appointed informers to ingratiate themselves to the new regime by spying on colleagues and reporting half-truths and outright false information—sometimes just to settle old scores! It was a confusing situation so I had decided to keep my plan to leave Iran a secret.

That morning when my ride to the airport arrived, Sherry was still in bed half asleep. I kissed her and told her that I would see her soon. She had no idea that I was not planning to return to Iran. I went to Mike's room where he was asleep and kissed his innocent face. I stayed there a minute looking at his colorful cartoon wallpaper wondering if I would be able to raise him in the United States, away from religious dictatorship and help him reach his potential as a human being; I had absolutely no idea how I would be able to do that. The night before, we had one of those usual family gatherings at my sister's home where I said goodbye to people I loved—my mom, dad, sister, brother, and other family members. I wasn't sure if or when I might see them again. Everyone thought I was going to New York City on a business trip but I was planning to stay in New York to visit BBDO and then fly to Portland, Oregon. I was uncertain about what I was going to do after that with my very limited savings. When I arrived in New York and checked in to the UN Plaza Hotel where BBDO international partners stayed, I called Sherry and asked her to sell everything and leave Iran immediately. She was shocked, but after a long pause, she accepted. Later, I learned that she arranged a big garage sale and everything was sold or given away including my nice suits and Mike's toys! Sherry told me the next day that the small grocer, the vegetable shop owner, and the milkman were all uncharacteristically well-dressed thanks to the expensive suits I had bought in London. She sold my Buick but my parents continued to live in the house that we had bought together for the next 10 years since I didn't want to disturb their lives by selling the house.

The next day at the BBDO headquarters in New York, I met some of the most important people in the advertising world. Tom Watson, a BBDO vice president, welcomed me and I met Bruce Crawford, the president of BBDO who warmly asked me if I wanted to work for them. I was honored by the casual suggestion, but in the back of my mind, I was thinking that the best place for peace and tranquility for myself and my family would be my house in West Linn, Oregon, near the beautiful Willamette River. I got an opportunity to chat with Allen Rosenshine, a creative icon who came across as a supersharp and articulate person; I wasn't surprised that he became the chairman and chief executive officer of BBDO, and later founded the Omnicom Group, the second largest advertising agency in the world.

During my stay in New York, I wanted to see how they managed a small advertising agency in the US so Tom arranged a day visit for me at one of their affiliates in Rochester, New York. I was surprised to see how similar their operations were to ours in Iran. I also visited the Ad Council in New York City; I always admired the way they harnessed the power of advertising to educate the public on topics ranging from child safety to emergency preparedness.

The last evening in New York, Bruce Crawford and his wife invited me to dinner at the iconic Four Season's Restaurant. I got there a little early and had my favorite drink, a Tom Collins, at the bar. Mr. Crawford came across as a warm, no-nonsense person. We talked about what was happening in Iran; my sense was that based on past experience, the most extreme and brutal groups usually come to power in post-revolutionary periods.

We both knew there wasn't much hope for my international clients to return to Iran soon. After dinner, they gave me a ride in their limo back to my hotel and when we said goodbye, it hit me that I was no longer a managing director. I felt the pain of leaving behind a decade of my professional life. I was a nobody in America. I must, however, admit that my mere relationship with BBDO indirectly helped me quite a bit in launching my new life in the United States and I am grateful for that.

During the flight to Portland, Oregon, I had a conversation with the young woman sitting next to me, a schoolteacher in Portland who mentioned that her husband was laid off and was spending his time collecting supermarket coupons at home. I was surprised but soon learned that the country was gripped with a simultaneous deep recession and high inflation, phenomenon known as stagflation, and many people were unemployed in the Portland area. A friend picked me up at the airport, and I bought a car a few days later. As I was driving the new Volvo off the dealership lot, "Rise" by Herb Alpert was playing on the radio and it was so inspiring! I was feeling blessed to be in the United States since Sherry and Mike were to join me soon, after a tumultuous year. The house in West Linn was about 25 minutes from downtown Portland.

Unlike most places we had lived, there were no fences between the houses. When Sherry and Mike arrived, we became friends with our neighbors. Our next-door neighbor was particularly kind and helped me lay a drainage pipe and cut wood after a big storm. I was developing some social and professional contacts, all of which came to a screeching halt when a group of Marxist students attacked the American embassy in Tehran on November 4, 1979, and took more than 50 Americans hostage. Unfortunately, instead of rescuing the hostages, Khomeini decided to publicly support the militants by sending his own son, Ahmad, to scale the embassy wall. I had a sense that the Soviets hammered a final coffin nail into the US-Iranian relations with their militant supporters in Iran. This was probably the first indication that Carter's naïve support of the Islamic Republic had backfired, putting Iran on a path to fall squarely into the hands of America's number one adversary in the world at that time—the Soviet Union. Of course, occupying the embassy and holding hostages was a badge of honor for the ruling Shia clerics among extremist militants inside and outside of Iran. They now had earned undisputable credentials as the enemy of the United States and gained the trust and respect of all anti-American and anti-Israeli groups in the region.

ABC dedicated *Nightline* to the coverage of the American hostages in Iran. We watched Ted Kopple with horror every night to learn about the hostage news that was so hot that it became the main staple of Ted Turner's Cable News Network (CNN) coverage. It was clear that the hostage crisis put Iran and the US on a collision course. It also created distance between most Iranians and Americans in the country. Overnight, Iranians lost the American goodwill that the shah had developed over decades. Unfortunately, the bad news out of Iran continued when, in late April of 1980, the US Army's attempt to rescue the 52 hostages in Iran (Eagle Claw) had failed and eight American servicemen and one Iranian civilian were killed when a helicopter collided with a transport airplane. The Iranian regime displayed the gruesome charcoaled bodies of the servicemen in front of the old US embassy building in Takht-e-Jamshid Avenue near my old high school, Iran Mehr.

Khomeini called the mission failure by the Delta Force an act of God that protected the Iranian Islamic regime. Again, the news for Iranians abroad was devastating. The event coupled with the hostage news got tremendous coverage.

It was an awful time to be an Iranian in America. The hostage news was everywhere and we couldn't get away from it. I was worried about the impact of all the shocking news on Sherry who was due in August 1980 with our sweet Melody. During her previous pregnancy, she had her mother, aunts, and her entire family by her side, but this time around, she had no family or close friends to support her and was constantly bombarded with ugly news from Iran. The picture of a mob of scruffy people chanting "death to America" in front of the US embassy was a fixture like a bookmark on most television stations.

I decided to take advantage of my free time and pursue a master's degree at the University of Portland, a Jesuit school. When I was filling out the application, I was confused by the race question as it was the first time anyone asked about my race. I didn't seem to fit into the given categories and the admissions clerk told me that based on government categories, individuals with ancestry from the Middle East are considered white. Later I found out that Employment Opportunity Commission regulations also explicitly defined as white original people of Europe, North Africa, and the Middle East— I thought that was a strange definition of whiteness. I was accepted into the master's program and started studying in the department of communication and creative arts. The program had a strong interpersonal component and went beyond just advertising. I was fascinated when we explored Martin Buber's ideas of I-Thou, suggesting that a genuine human communication takes place when two people actively engage each other, as he put it, in "here and now" as opposed to not fully being present during interactions.

At the University of Portland, I was introduced to Marshal McLuhan's idea that the nature of medium apart from its content has the power of reshaping social life. Although he was talking about television, he could have very well predicted the impact of social media in his famous saying of "the medium is the message." I was happy that I had decided to enroll in the program and in May of 1980, I received my master's degree in communication from the University of Portland. Mike was there and so was Melody, albeit in Sherry's tummy. That MA degree from a US university meant a lot to me, especially since I had left the US about a decade earlier without a degree and had always felt guilty about that.

My professor and advisor Robert Fulford encouraged me to go to the University of Washington in Seattle to pursue a doctorate degree, something that I had never thought about. A couple of weeks later, I drove to Seattle and met with Professor Alex Edelstein, the chair of the school of communication. He was interested in my background and told me that I should take the graduate record examination and Miller's Analogy Test and get back to him. In the meantime. I wrote a letter to Tom Watson of BBDO and asked if there was a possibility that I could work for them, preferably in an international setting.

As we were enjoying the beautiful May weather in Oregon, I noticed that our front lawn and car parked on the driveway were covered with snow. I told Sherry that it was so strange to have snow in Oregon in May! It wasn't snow. It was volcanic ash from Mount St. Helen that had just erupted after frequently shaking the ground and steaming. It erupted several more times and always spewed ashes. One day, as I was driving to the University of Portland on Willamette Boulevard, I saw one of the most spectacular volcanic eruptions of Mt. St. Helen spewing ash from about 60 miles away. On the radio in the car, people were reporting the eruption from multiple vantage points. Without a doubt, depending on where people come from, they see things differently, and that is always the challenge in communication. That summer, I locked myself in a room and went over as many as GRE tests that I could lay my hands on. I also studied for Miller's Analogies Test, which was hard. I passed the tests and was accepted into the communication doctoral program at the University of Washington. That meant we had to move to Seattle shortly after Melody's birth in August.

Sherry was getting a bit heavy and somewhat homesick; adding insult to injury, she had to wear a mask to avoid breathing the volcanic ash that permeated the Portland area. Around June, I took her and Mike to the beautiful Rose Festival in Portland. I knew Sherry would enjoy the event since she loves flowers. We also visited the warships and submarines that annually anchor at Portland's waterfront during the festival. The whole thing was so new to Mike and he really liked the tall warships. It felt we were connecting with America through the festival that, with its flowers, music, and pageantry was lifting our spirits.

In August of 1980, Melody was born in Portland Good Samaritan Hospital and Sherry and I were delighted to have a beautiful girl. She was so pretty that it melted my heart when I saw her for the first time. We had a very short window to move to Seattle and the real estate market was terrible. As a last resort, I sold the West Linn home to a prominent Iranian architect on contract; because he lacked a credit history, he was not able to obtain a mortgage. He gave me a down payment and we had a formal agreement that he would make monthly payments, and after two years, he would make a balloon payment for the remainder of his debt. He told me he was going to Iran to sell his properties.

Seattle is three hours from Portland, both cities are absolutely gorgeous places to live and both enjoy a lush forestry. Portland has Willamette, Columbia, and Clackamas Rivers, while Seattle is home to Lake Washington, Lake Union, and Lake Sammamish. With the sale of the Oregon home, I bought a new home in Bellevue Washington and a few friends helped us move into it. It was a four-bedroom house with the perfect view of beautiful Lake Sammamish from most rooms. The pine trees around the lake created a breathtaking view like that of Lake Tahoe.

For most of the next three-and-a-half years, I drove on the Evergreen Point Floating Bridge over Lake Washington on my way to and from the university a few miles north of downtown Seattle. The one-and-a-half-mile bridge was the longest floating bridge in the world at the time. It felt like I was in a boat when driving on the bridge. Going over the bridge in the morning charged my mental energies for the day, and in the evening, helped me decompress and relax. I loved the University of Washington's campus—the buildings with mixed architectural styles and a Gothic flavor gave a strong sense of pure academia and learning, especially the communications building that reminded me of a monastery where you could isolate yourself and focus on knowledge. The school was a truly cutting-edge educational environment for intellectual growth and research. It initially seemed a bit impersonal and too structured when compared to the University of Portland, but as time went on, professors seemed warmer and more supportive. There was much focus on empirical research and communication theory. Most of the time, I tried to anecdotally correspond some of the theoretical ideas to my personal and professional experiences.

I took a class with Professor Dick Carter who was, in my opinion, a great thinker and had trailblazing ideas about communication research. Every week, Carter gave us an article from *Science Magazine* dealing with some transformative scientific discoveries like the invention of lightbulb or telephone and assigned a chapter from *The Conduct of Inquiry,* a book by Abraham Kaplan who was a clinical psychologist and philosopher of science. The book was organized into chapters dealing with philosophical aspects of topics like concepts, theories, laws, and experiments, among others. We had to write a two-page paper linking the assigned chapter in the book with the assigned magazine article. For the first assignment, I was thinking about it all week but could not produce even a word that I felt was relevant. It was a hard class, but the challenge was most enjoyable. I had always disliked statistics and managed to avoid taking it, but once I understood the concept of measurement and data matrix, I took an advanced class with Professor Allen Edwards who wrote the book *Multiple Regression and the Analysis of Variance and Covariance* and fell in love with quantitative research. For my social psychology class, I used to punch cards to prepare data for statistical analysis with software packages on mainframe computers.

Around the student union where I went for coffee, there was always a group of Iranian students distributing pamphlets and other propaganda materials in support of the Islamic Republic of Iran during the Iran–Iraq War. Some were sympathizers of People's Mujaheddin who later clashed with the Islamic Republic and assassinated a score of their leaders, including Beheshti and Bahonar, whom I had met in Iran. Subsequently, hardcore members of People's Mujaheddin escaped to Iraq and sided with Saddam Hussein in the war against Iran. In turn, the Islamic Republic executed thousands of their members, including many young men and women who had naively associated themselves with the People's Mujaheddin. The group operated in Iraq until the fall of Saddam's regime. I heard in 2021 they were in Albany, a very small country in Eastern Europe, with a 57 percent Muslim population.

As the Iran–Iraq War raged, my parents reported the daily rain of Iraqi Scud missiles and dumb bombs on residential parts of Tehran. My mom mentioned they were in high spirits but had to frequently stop their gin rummy card game and go to the basements for shelter. I had no idea that even Mike, a five-year-old boy, was following the war on CNN. One day, he told me happily that we were winning the war. I tried to move him away from the subject, but when I was reading a book for him at night, he told me with a sad face that we were now losing. That day, Mike had learned from CNN that Saddam Hussein had taken Khorramshahr, a strategic port south of Iran in oil-rich Khuzestan province at the confluence of the Arvand and Karun Rivers. He also bombed the Abadan Refinery, the largest in the world and a catastrophic defeat for the Iranian forces at the time. I quickly limited Mike's TV watching to *Sesame Street*, *Mr. Rogers*, and some benign cartoons to slowly get him out of thinking about the war in Iran. Before he went to kindergarten, I decided to give him an

American name so he could easily blend in. I asked him what he liked for a middle name; he liked to be called Mike, so his legal name was changed Mike Farbod Zandpour when he was 18 years old and became a US citizen.

Just as I was beginning to feel comfortable in Washington and in response to a letter I had sent a couple of months before, Tom Watson called and asked if I was ready to go to work for BBDO. I was honored by the offer and it would have been great news for me about a month earlier, but I was deeply involved with my new life and was hesitant to give it up. After talking with Sherry, I decided to tell him that my plan was to complete my PhD, although I knew refusing a rare offer like that was quite risky since there was no guarantee that I would be granted a PhD or land an academic job in the United States, but as an eternal optimist, I was hopeful!

In late October of 1982, Alex Edelstein asked me to go to Washington, DC, to participate in a program sponsored by the United States Information Agency (USIA). I stayed with a USIA contact person who was in the Army Core of Engineers and living with her husband in DC. It was a fun trip and there were students from Germany, Greece, France, and so on. As part of the program, they took us to a symphony concert at the Kennedy Center where Secretary of State George Shultz was also attending. The program provided a number of speakers who discussed different aspects of government communication. The most surprising thing to me was our visit to the old Blackies House of Beef Déjà Vu Cocktail Lounge that was in the old courtyard where I had worked during a summer about 15 or 16 years earlier. It was indeed a real déjà vu! That was surreal and took me back to my first visit to the US.

With all the cognitive and research stuff, I was getting a little off track. With an eye on the job market, I decided to combine my advertising experience with my new research skills and theoretical knowledge in communication. To keep a foot in advertising was a good strategy since there were many university job openings for advertising faculty. The title of my proposal for my dissertation was "Cognitive Response to Political Advertising." Richard Carter, my de facto advisor, invited me and fellow students Michael Nilan and Tom Jacobson to attend a mini conference that had been arranged by his former student Steven Chafee, now chair of the department of communication at Stanford University in California. A few days before our trip, Carter arranged a session to practice our presentation. It was so hard to present several months of intense work in just 10 minutes—I was so attached to every word and every sentence that it seemed impossible to let them go.

Carter drove us in his old car to California while we engaged in several hot debates about a variety of topics. The mini conference went quite well and doctoral students from a few other universities were present. Professor Chaffee and his wife had a nice reception for the group at their home.

Right after my dissertation defense before Thanksgiving of 1983, my in-laws visited from Iran. They were so happy to see Mike after several years and Melody for the first time. In 1984, while my in-laws were still visiting, the US designated Iran as the sponsor of terrorism and put an arms embargo on Iran. When I took them to SEA-TAC airport to depart for Tehran, their Iran Air tickets were no longer honored, and I had to buy Japan Airlines ticket for them to get home.

I had left Iran, but the events there were following me everywhere. First there was the chaotic Islamic Revolution, then American embassy hostage crisis and the US failed rescue attempt of the hostages, then the Iran–Iraq stupid and brutal war that killed at least a million people, and finally, the terrorism designation. The war was still raging and we regularly heard heartbreaking stories of brutalities. For example, Sherry's maternal cousin Ali, a bright, good-natured boy was snatched from school and forced into a bus traveling to the front line in support of the Islamic Republic military. Government clergy was making them psychologically ready by exalting all the virtues of martyrdom that is part of the Shia culture. When Ali was in a foxhole during an attack, an Iraqi soldier showed up above him. Ali shot the soldier who was wounded badly and fell on top of him in the hole before he died. During the night, Ali looked at the soldier's wallet and saw a picture of the man's wife and children. Ali felt very guilty and sad; he endured the weight of the dead soldier all night. Later, he became quite depressed and eventually committed suicide. There are many stories like that.

I graduated in March of 1984 and taught an advertising class for a couple of quarters before I found a tenure-track job. I had told Professor Larry Bowen, the head of the advertising program, that I would be happy to teach any of the advertising courses except what the copy and layout class, but lo and behold, I was assigned a section of the copy and layout class! Still, I was excited that the class would give me some teaching experience and it was a paid assignment. It was the first time I would earn money for work since I left Iran in 1979.

My first day of teaching didn't go smoothly. I had decided to look my best by wearing one of the few nice suits that I had brought from Iran about five years earlier, not realizing that I had gained a few pounds since. About 15 minutes before class, my trousers' zipper went off track. It was an awful situation for my teaching debut, not to mention that I would be the laughingstock of students all year. I rushed to Pat Dinning, our graduate secretary who was very nice and gave me a safety pin to temporarily fix it. Fortunately, it was partially covered by my long jacket but as I was picking up my Samsonite briefcase a couple of minutes before class, my jacket's button fell off and left me with absolutely no protection. I had no choice but to hold the briefcase in front of me as I entered the classroom. I went straight to the slant-top lectern and was determined to stay there the entire time. As I was going through the roster, my pen on the top of the lectern rolled down and fell a few feet away. I needed it but could not pick it up without exposing myself, so to speak. I am sure students were wondering why I was glued to the lectern the whole time. After, despite several students asking questions, I finally managed to use my briefcase as a shield and get out of the classroom after every student had left. The class went nicely for the rest of the quarter. I had great students including a Huskie who had been recruited by the National Football League.

I had applied to several universities for a tenure-track teaching position in advertising and anxiously checked my voicemail every day for a possible interview invitation. Around July of 1984 when Sherry and I were visiting her college friend Mitra in Redwood City, California, I got a message that Dean Mills, the director of the School of Communication at Penn State University wanted me to be there by Sunday afternoon for a Monday and Tuesday interview. I immediately took my jackets and trousers for dry cleaning and paid extra to have them back before 5 p.m. When we went to pick up my clothes around 4:45, the place was closed! Sherry and I were shocked and I was trying not to panic but my flight was early Sunday morning and most clothing stores were closing. A friend, Ahmad, had suits that were a perfect fit, but his trousers were a few inches too long for me. Sherry and her friend went to work and fixed the trousers and prepared a couple of nice suits and ties for my interview.

After dinner that evening, our friends told their horrifying story of leaving Iran during the Iraq war and traveling to the United States. They had paid half of a hefty fee in advance and the other half when they reached Spain. They were moved by a vast network of people in Iran, Turkey, and Europe who would help Iranians flee Iran. Our friends and their two young children traveled on the back of motorbikes and mules and had walked most nights as they were handed from one armed group to another for days until they reached Europe where they finally obtained a US visa.

CHAPTER 6

Becoming an Advertising Professor in the United States

The next day I was at State College, which was a bit isolated and I had to transfer to smaller commuter plane to get there. Dean Mills and his two sons picked me up from the airport and took me to the Nittany Lion Inn. The next day, I made a research presentation at the Carnegie Hall where the school of communication was located but most faculty members were old journalists with little appreciation for quantitative research. I had a nice dinner with Dean Mills and Professor John Pavlik at Victoria Manor restaurant and a deep philosophical discussion about the limits of the First Amendment, Dean's favorite topic.

After I got home, I was offered the job and I immediately took it. I was so excited to teach advertising in a major university in the US! We had a little time before the start of the academic year so I decided to drive leisurely to see the country up close. After a large garage sale and several goodbye parties, we were on our way to our new life. We were amazed by the natural beauty of Idaho, where we spent the night. Melody was about four and wanted to go home; she was asking about her friends and the swing set in our backyard. I could see tears in Sherry's eyes. It was sweet that we were going to a new life, but once again, we were leaving friends and favorite places behind. I was driving most of the day, east on I-90 toward Yellowstone National Park. It was getting dark so we decided to stay over in a little town called Nevada City, Montana. We checked into a hotel that looked a bit antique, but it was dark and everyone was too tired to pay attention to the surroundings. When we got up in the morning, it felt like we had traveled back in time—everything in the hotel was old! Nevada City was a ghost town from the gold rush era around 1880 and had been kept mostly intact for tourists. We checked the museum and saw the old post office, school, sheriff's office, jail, grocery store, and so on. We were lucky to experience a bit of the old West. We spent the next couple of days in Yellowstone National Park and saw its famous geysers, hot springs, and other natural marvels. I read the park's literature and couldn't help but admire President Ulysses Grant's vision for signing the 1872 Yellowstone National Park Protection Act; in so doing, he created the first US national park.

Soon, we were at Keystone State. I had forgotten how beautiful the trees were on the East Coast in early fall. We were finally in State College that is known as Happy Valley. I traded my Volvo for a Chevrolet station wagon since we were planning to make many trips to the Washington DC area and needed a bigger car. We rented a house from a meteorology professor who was spending his sabbatical year with his family in France. We had never lived in anybody else's house but it was an interesting place with many books and games. They also had quite a few stringed instruments since they played historical music in a band. Part of the deal was to take care of their old, one-eyed cat. We never had cats and didn't quite know how to deal with it. The first night, it hid under one of the beds and would not come out. The next morning, it came out and slowly got used to us. Every night at exactly at the same time, he signaled that he wanted to come in by scratching the screen. The children's bedroom was on the other side of the single-level house so Mike and Melody wanted me to "guard" them by spending time and telling stories before they went to sleep. The day after we moved into the house in State College, we saw four eyes peep through the mail slot. They were two little girls, Mary and Mika, daughters of our neighbor who was a campus minister. They soon became Melody's best friends. They had a brother about the same age as Mike and they all went to Radio Park Elementary School together.

One of the early friends at Penn State University was Vince Norris who had just published research about *MAD* magazine suggesting media may be able to survive without advertising. Vince and his wife introduced us to a group of faculty members and spouses who got together in a dark basement in College Avenue every Friday evening. There was a keg of beer, everyone brought salads and other munchies, and we had lots of interesting conversations. We would go out with a few of the younger faculty on weekends.

I met a Polish journalist who was presenting to the Penn State journalism faculty about the solidarity movement in Poland and the heroic efforts its leader, Lech Walesa, who later became the president of Poland. He and his wife seemed like a nice, friendly couple. One day, I noticed there was a sign close to my office about a bomb threat and most people had left the building. One of my colleagues told me he had seen this sign a few times and it was a hoax. We both ignored it, but later the Polish journalist showed up at my office door and told me jokingly that he was not surprised to see that I wasn't afraid of the bomb. When I asked him why, he responded by saying that most Iranians knew how to disarm a bomb. That statement loudly spoke of the stereotypical image Americans had of Iranians created by the behavior of the Islamic Republic and the media during 1980s.

During our first year at Penn State University when Melody was about four, Sherry took an overnight out-of-town trip to participate in a ping pong tournament. Before she left, she emphatically asked me to be sure to give Melody her breakfast. When we got up in the morning, I made the breakfast that consisted of scrambled eggs, milk, and toast. Mike ate his breakfast but Melody refused to eat after her first bite. I put Melody in the guest room and told her when she was done with her breakfast she could come out and play. After about three or four minutes, she came out and showed me the empty plate. I kissed and hugged her and she went out to play. Years later, she told me she dumped the eggs in the waste basket in that room because the eggs were too salty—my eggs did not taste like Mom's! I felt bad that I had not asked her why she was not eating her breakfast before I gave her the time-out.

The following year, we moved to an old house close to campus. It was the only rental that we could find. One evening after having a few beers with my colleague in a nearby bar, I was walking home and my nose and ears felt frozen. I had forgotten how cold it could get during winters on the East Coast.

During a blizzard once, someone dropped an envelope through the mail slot. I was surprised that anyone was out there in that weather. It was a citation; my colleague and neighbor, Tom Berner, who was also a city councilman told me the borough ordinance required residents clean up the snow from their sidewalk before it freezes. He had a blower and came to my rescue whenever it snowed.

A few nights later, after we put the kids in bed, we heard what sounded like an explosion in the basement. The old WWII-era furnace shut off and the temperature inside the house was dropping by the minute. I had no idea how to fix it so we started to put the blankets, clothing, and even rugs on the kids to keep them warm. I was getting a bit unhappy in the Happy Valley—we were missing the mild weather of the northwest!

While at Penn State University, I received a grant for looking into use of media and decisional processes during the 1986 gubernatorial election campaign. The candidates were Democrat Bob Casey and Republican Bill Scranton. We interviewed a random panel of Pennsylvania registered voters from precincts around the state before, during, and after the election. The results showed that a surprising two-thirds of all voters focused only on the candidate of their party and made up their minds early in the campaign, paid little attention to campaign messages, and didn't know much about the other candidate's personal characteristics and policies. In contrast, one-third of all voters engaged compared the two candidates, used more media, and had more knowledge about the campaign. These voters were less extreme in their attitudes and were more likely to switch candidates. Later, my paper won first place in the Western Communications Education Annual Conference in 1988 and was published in *Mass Comm Review* in 1989.

During my third academic year at Penn State University, one of my colleagues asked me to fly with him on his Cherokee airplane to Baton Rouge, Louisiana, where we both were presenting papers. I agreed and gave him the airline allowance the university paid me for presenting a paper that was accepted in a national conference. I had some reservations, since my colleague was a beer drinker, but he was a senior professor and I could not afford to get on his bad side. Additionally, I knew he was a good pilot. Someone mentioned that he had experience landing planes on aircraft carriers. On the day of travel, he called me and asked if Sherry could give us a ride to the airport. When we got in the car, we could smell alcohol on his breath from the back seat! Sherry told me in Farsi that it was not safe to fly with him but it was too late for me to back out.

Soon we arrived in front of a small remote hanger and when he opened the doors, I was surprised to see a very small plane sitting there—certainly not what I had imagined. I asked him if the plane had only one engine. He got a bit irritated and asked me how many engines my car had and whether it ever stopped during a ride with that one engine! I kept quiet, and as soon as we got in the small plane, he gave me a piece of paper to call out all the items that needed to be checked off. Before I knew it, we were airborne. He would tilt the plane toward my side, which made me quite uncomfortable, as I was looking down through the transparent window. He let me use the side control and instructed me how to fly. I loved it but that was the only time that I got so close to flying an airplane. We had many stops along the way and he explained to me how the radio system worked. When we got to Baton Rouge, I was very hungry and we went out to eat with a group of conference attendees. We went to a place that only served crawfish. I did not know how to eat it and had a very hard time getting anything out of the shell but pretended that I was doing okay.

The plane had room for five people so I wondered why our other two colleagues from the school of communication who were also presenting papers in Baton Rouge had not joined us. One told me that he flew with him the previous year, but due to a storm, they got stranded in some remote airport for a couple of days. He also gave me the unsettling news that the university insurance did not cover flights on private planes.

One night in Baton Rouge, the organizing committee arranged a tour of Nottoway Plantation where we saw a giant antebellum mansion with rooms overlooking the Mississippi River. The magnificent building located about 18 miles south of Baton Rouge had been built by slaves for John Randolph in the mid-1800s. We were welcomed as guests of the Randolph family would have been; they reenacted the entire evening like we were in the old days: Upon arrival, we were offered a glass of light, dry sherry as aperitif by a Black lady wearing a vintage dress, then another Black lady played a couple of plantation-era songs on the piano before serving a formal dinner like the old days. I thought the whole thing was racist and glorified the time of slavery, yet it was educational as it brought attention to the plight of the slaves and the whole ugliness of slavery. It was hard to see how people with such elegant taste who displayed genteel hospitality treated the enslaved with such horrible cruelty.

Still, becoming a US citizen was one of the great days for me and Sherry. On May 22, 1986, Sherry and I went to Center Court in Bellefonte, Pennsylvania, a small town nearby, to attend our naturalization oath ceremony. As we descended the steps to the basement for our usual Friday evening faculty gathering in College Avenue that night, our friends started cheering and congratulating us. They had seen us on the front page of the local newspaper, *Center Daily Times*, taking the oath of allegiance to the United States; it was such a joyful day. As Fred and Sherry, our new legal names, we were ready for a celebration with our fellow Americans! I remember President Reagan's words that as a foreigner, you could never call yourself German in Germany or Japanese in Japan, but you could call yourself American in the United States.

Shortly after we became US citizens, we invited Sherry's younger brother, Saeed, to visit. We were so happy to see him, especially since he had been arrested by the Islamic regime and subjected to severe flogging, the evidence was all over his back! He had very little financial resources but was a capable man. I suggested that he study engineering, but he was determined to get into business for himself in the Los Angeles area where we had quite a few family members. I also suggested that he change his first name to Simon to better blend into the business community. He worked hard for many years in the apparel business. Several years into the business, his using Swarovski crystals on belts became a phenomenal success, especially after Madonna wore one while performing at a concert. He manufactured the belts in the United States under his brand name, B.B. Simon, with annual revenues in the millions. He is a testament that America is indeed the land of opportunity for those who have innovative ideas and are willing to work hard to make them a reality!

At Penn State, longtime coach of the Nittany Lions, Joe Paterno, was worshipped by everyone at the university and beyond. He lived an unpretentious lifestyle near our home. I was surprised to see huge crowds that came from all over Pennsylvania to support the Nittany Lions. Tailgating was a big event during home games and countless recreational vehicles converged on University Park where entire families cheered for the home team. Even senior professors were anxious about the results of the games, not to mention the fundraising folks in the development office. I heard the fundraising numbers were quite high after a victory.

People drank a lot of alcohol during home games and anger and unruliness increased when the Nittany Lions lost. A police officer with whom I was working on a grant proposal told me that after a defeat, they received a higher number of complaints about domestic disturbances, including assault and battery. Paterno in his dark glasses was a fixture of the games, always pacing with anxiety on the side of the field.

Unfortunately, with all that glory he had a tragic ending. In 2011, we learned that his assistant, Jerry Sandusky, had been engaging in criminal child sexual abuse at the university for the prior 15 years but nobody had reported it to the police! I was especially disgusted since it happened while I was teaching at Penn State. Sandusky was sentenced to a minimum of 30 years in prison, many university management staff were fired, and Jo Paterno was criticized for not informing the police. Despite student riots in his favor, he was fired and his statue was removed from the campus. One of my son's classmates in sixth and seventh grades, Mike McQueary, who played football with Mike during recess, became an assistant coach to Paterno and was the first Penn State employee to report Sandusky, but the university fired him to cover it up. Fortunately, when the facts became known, the university had to settle his lawsuit by paying him around $12 million!

*****

It was incredibly unfortunate that the coverage of bad news from the Islamic Republic was never-ending. Other constant news coverage was the Iran-Contra affair that involved the sale of anti-tank Tows and surface-to-air Hawk missiles to the Islamic Republic of Iran, which was under arms embargo by the United States. Proceeds from the arms sales were illegally transferred to the Contras, a coalition of right-wing rebel groups fighting the Sandinista Marxist regime in Nicaragua. Various congressional investigations and court proceedings were on the news for months, keeping the Iran name front and center in the world every day.

We all needed a break from the bad news that was directly affecting my family. I had promised Mike and Melody we'd go to Disney World in Florida during the winter break of 1986. Our travel date was the day after Christmas and after we all opened our presents, we were ready to hit the road. I backed the car out of the garage and was putting our luggage in our station wagon when the heavy garage door of the old house accidentally dropped on the car like a guillotine and crushed the tailgate. I was shocked that the garage door had no sensor. It was a total disaster. Melody and Mike would be heartbroken since they had been looking forward to our trip for months. There was no way that I could renege on my promise. I started frantically looking for a rental car in State College on foot. The small town looked deserted as the students had gone home for the holidays. Most places were closed, but I kept trying until I found a gas station that had a car for rent and soon were on our way to Orlando,

Florida. I met my cousin, Shane, and his friend there. We were invited to celebrate the New Year at a lavish party in a waterfront mansion that belonged to a Columbian friend of a friend of my cousin. Many young people were already there when we arrived, but the host didn't really know anyone and was talking only to a couple of people. Still, we all had so much fun during that trip, especially Mike and Melody who loved Disney World.

*****

As charming as our small town was, I was beginning to feel isolated. Contrary to what I had initially thought, it was a long trip to Philadelphia or Washington DC on narrow roads, especially in winter. Air travel was quite inconvenient since only small planes could fly in and out of State College Airport. Most importantly, my salary was too low and it was hard to support my family. I was not enjoying the divisive school environment under the new dean either; I was glad I hadn't bought a house there and had no long-term commitment. One day, an older faculty friend mentioned that most children of professors leave the area to attend college in large metropolitan areas and to find work while the parents are stuck in State College. That reminded me of our next-door neighbor who had once been a chair of physics department but he and his elderly wife could hardly go anywhere and seldom did any family visit them. They loved their home and their beautiful flowers; it was so sad that they had to leave everything to go to a retirement home. I liked State College, Pennsylvania, but wasn't planning to grow old there.

Bad news kept coming out of Iran. President Ronald Regan ordered Operation Praying Mantis in April of 1988 that destroyed most of the Iranian navy in Iranian territorial waters of the Persian Gulf in retaliation for the Iranians damaging an American warship and mining international waters. On July 3, the USS *Vincennes* shot down Iran Air flight 655 with a surface-to-air missile of the US Navy. The Airbus A300 had just taken off from Bandar Abbas with 290 passengers onboard. Both countries accused each other of miscommunication and negligence, but the images of scattered passenger belongings on the Persian Gulf waters brought tears to the eyes of Iranians and Americans alike.

Most of our family members were in Southern California, especially in Orange County. My brother, Farrokh, had just moved to Newport Beach from Big Bear Lake where he had been a physician in the community hospital for several years. Around that time, I heard Cal State Fullerton University was searching for an advertising faculty; I was immediately interested and applied for a tenure-track associate professor. The university seemed especially attractive since it was in the second largest media market in the United States and part of the Cal State University System, one of the largest in the world. When I was invited for an interview, I decided to stay with my brother and his family for a couple of weeks and check out Cal State Fullerton and a few other universities. Farrokh had an extra car, a Jeep Cherokee, that I drove. I wasn't used to the Southern California freeway system and it seemed a bit complicated to me at first. Once, I was running late for an appointment in Long Beach and as I was searching for the address, I found myself on top of Gerald Desmond Bridge and had no idea how to get off it!

When I went back to State College, I received an offer from Cal State Fullerton as an associate professor in their tenure-track program. I had to report to work in January of 1988 if I wanted to take the job. Sherry needed to be at Penn State University until April to complete her master's thesis in educational psychology. We decided that she would stay with the kids until she was done. We also arranged for the furniture to be sent to our new home. Our neighbor Tom Berner organized a little reception to say farewell when I was leaving. A few of my colleagues, John Pavlik, Susan Strohm, and her husband, came. I put all my books, typewriter, etc., in the back of my car and got on my way to California in the middle of winter. After driving for a few hours, I noticed the road ahead was getting dark and soon I found myself in the middle of a blizzard. I checked into a motel where a couple of Indian families were sitting in the lobby. The next day, everything was buried in such deep snow that I had a hard time finding my car. There were quite a few bridge closures and other delays along the way; driving in Arkansas was particularly hazardous since they had been unable to clear the snow before it froze. I met a truck driver along the way who needed to talk to someone and had opinions about everything from beating the stock market to the future of the world.

Finally, after several grueling days, I arrived at my brother's house in Corona Delmar, Newport Beach. I needed to find a place for our family to live but California real estate was hot; when I was looking at a small condominium during an open house in Irvine, the agent told me they already received three offers. The rental market was just as bad but I eventually managed to rent a three-bedroom condo a few miles away from the university in a subdivision across from Tri-City Park on Kramer's Blvd. in Placentia. We had access to a nice pool and the beautiful park.

During shah's time in Iran, Sherry's last position in the ministry of education was testing exceptional students and she was involved in standardizing aptitude and IQ test projects. She always wanted to pursue her education and she finally got her opportunity at Penn State University. I was so happy that she was intellectually engaged and advanced her knowledge in an area that she had always liked. Soon, Sherry and the kids joined me. Mike discarded his quarter-size violin for a half-size violin. The kids had a good music teacher at Tuffree Middle School who sometimes had them play in nursing homes in Placentia. I thought it was a wonderful idea since the kids brought so much joy to the older people, but sometimes their "music" sounded like anything but. Some of the residents looked at the kids as though they were reminded of their own grandkids. We always went to watch the kids play and it was funny how the older people in the nursing homes would quarrel over a chair just like little kids. Melody was taking acoustic guitar lessons and later a neighbor's daughter, Melony Strunk, encouraged her to sign up for dance classes. Melody was making good progress and we went to see her perform.

We were feeling at home with so many family members nearby in Orange County, including my two brothers and their families, Sherry's two brothers and their families, and countless cousins. We were busy and developed very few friendships outside of the university and our extended family. Melody went to Mariposa Elementary School and then Brea Junior High School. Eventually, both Mike and Melody attended Brea Olinda High School.

I heard President Regan was coming to a rally at Cal State Fullerton to support George H. Bush for president. In addition to my interest in political communication, I wanted to see Reagan. A handful of people were at the rally in the gym sitting on the floor, but soon the place was packed and it was standing room only. Without remembering how it got there, I had a balloon in my right hand and a placard with the picture of George H. Bush in the other hand. As soon as Regan appeared on the stage, the mood was electric. He started by saying "Orange County is the home of all good Republicans," and everyone raised their balloons and placards and shouted something like "Bush for president!" This went on for the next 45 minutes; there was no way I could not participate enthusiastically among that crowd, so I raised the balloon and the poster frequently like everyone else.

In 1989, I was appointed head of the advertising program, which was among the largest in the country with more than 1,100 undergraduate majors. Now, I had the opportunity to make some constructive changes in the program. I often wondered why so many students chose the advertising major despite the shrinking job market. The demand for the advertising major was so high that many programs were turning down applicants. In 1990, five thousand students were expected to graduate with an advertising degree but less than half would find a job. Many agencies were laying off people. I guess some of the advertising students were just transferring from business programs to advertising to avoid calculus and other mathematics requirements. Others were attracted to the seeming glitz and glamour of advertising and some were truly talented. In August 1990, Bruce Horovitz from the *Los Angeles Times* interviewed me and my students for an article in which he was highlighting the issue. He said Paul Del Pizzo, a student in my class, told him hopelessly he "probably would be selling pizza in Laguna Niguel, instead of working in Madison Avenue selling images!"

I wanted to make sure we did everything to make our students more marketable. Fortunately, several supportive advertising faculty members helped me make some useful changes. The first was to create an advertising writing class, replacing the old report-writing one that trained students to look for facts instead of working with their own imagination. We also changed the name of the class "Copy and Layout" to "Strategy and Execution," opening the door to teaching strategic thinking for multimedia applications. We created an advanced creative course for students to build a creative portfolio to show employers. We acquired a homegrown media planning software for students to use in the computer labs, calculating reach and frequency as well as the cost effectiveness of their advertising media plans. In addition, we asked students to take management and marketing or studio art classes to complement their knowledge, depending on their area of interest. It was ironic that while about 70 percent of our advertising students were females at that time, we had an all-male advertising faculty. As part of my job, I searched for and facilitated the hiring of several highly qualified female professionals as adjunct and full-time faculty members.

In early 1989, the spread of HIV and AIDS was becoming a growing public health problem. Susan Sullivan, a public health nurse and AIDS education coordinator at the Orange County chapter of the American Red Cross invited me to join a health care subcommittee as a volunteer expert for their public awareness and education campaigns about AIDS. Susan Sullivan was quite passionate about educating the public about AIDS and the committee met every week in the Orange County Red Cross building. I knew AIDS was deadly but did not know much else. Most politicians and Orange County school districts avoided getting involved since AIDS was perceived to be "a gay disease" and no one wished to be associated with it in conservative Orange County. I remember everyone sitting on one side of the conference table during meetings—away from a committee member who had AIDS.

We decided to focus our efforts on developing an effective low-budget program to help prevent the spread of AIDS among youth. I suggested organizing a poster contest for teens in Orange County and Susan proposed that Orange County libraries could promote the idea and offer Red Cross educational materials about AIDS to youth visiting the libraries. Students would create a poster to educate their peers about AIDS based on the knowledge they acquired from the educational materials at the library. The posters to be included in the contest were sent to my address at Cal State Fullerton University and the project was a great success. Hundreds of posters entered the competition; I was amazed by the number and quality of the posters that we received. The committee selected the winners based on how creative and compelling the posters were. The best posters were displayed at the Fullerton Museum and the winners received their prizes at the museum on the annual AIDS Walk in Orange County. In an interview with the campus newspaper *Daily Titan* a few years later, Susan Sullivan talked about the history of the project and mentioned that it was continued at the University of California Irvine.

One of the interesting features of living in Southern California was seeing people from a variety of cultures all over the world. For example, when we were living in the city of Brea,

Sherry and I decided to have dinner at a restaurant close to our house while we were waiting for Melody to finish her dance rehearsal. As we entered the Indian restaurant, we heard Arabic music and saw an Asian lady belly dancing; at the table, a Mexican gentleman took our order. I told Sherry how amazing it was that two Iranians in the United States were watching an Asian woman dancing to Arabic music and were being served Indian food by a Mexican person. You couldn't make that up! At Cal State Fullerton, we also had a diverse international student body from Europe, Asia, and South and Central America. I would take my computer for repair to a Chinese man who was talking to me while exchanging information with someone in Chinese and fixing a device all at the same time, in contrast with American men who seemed they were not much into multitasking. I became interested in learning more about such differences.

As economic and technological forces continued to move the world closer to a single market in the early 1990s, there was an increasing demand for universal brand names, multilingual packaging, and uniform advertising across nations. There was no guide for how international advertisers should tailor their advertising to fit individual countries in terms of creative strategies and information levels. I thought this was a fertile area of research and it interested me.

Assuming national cultures are reflected in the television advertising of a country, I thought the messages in those ads may reflect similarities and differences among communication patterns in different cultures. Fortunately, the Department of Communication had many international students from a variety of countries who were also interested in the topic. I started with a comparative study of television commercials of the US, France, and Taiwan, which was also the master thesis for a couple of graduate students able to record a random sample of television commercials from the three countries. We investigated patterns in their creative strategies and the level of information provided to their audiences. The article "Stories, Symbols and Straight Talk" was published in the *Journal of Advertising Research* in 1992, the United States' premier periodical in the field.

As I continued that line of research with my students frm US, Taiwan, Korea, Germany, France, England, Spain and Mexico, we collected a random sample of about two thousand TV commercials from seven countries in Asia, Europe, and North America. It was by far the most exciting research work that I had done. We incorporated the work of Dutch social psychologist Greet Hofstede who had developed one of the earliest and most popular quantified dimensions of culture at a global level. We also included numerous control variables by incorporating the findings of others, such as the legal environment, governing advertising and similar issues into our study to ensure equivalency and eliminate alternative explanations. We finally developed a model consisting of 23 countries to address the growing need of global marketers to communicate effectively with people from a wide variety of national cultures. Our research was named top paper in the International Communication Annual Conference in Sydney, Australia, and we published it for the second time in the *Journal of Advertising Research* in 1994 with student co-authors and the title, "Global Reach and Local Touch: Achieving Cultural Fitness in TV Advertising." Later, in collaboration with my colleague professor Katrin Harich, we wrote an article titled "Think and Feel Country Clusters" that was published in 1996 in *the International Journal of*

Advertising, the United Kingdom premier research journal in the field. In 2005, the *Journal of Advertising* named me among the top 10 most cited researchers in the field of international advertising between 1990 and 2002, based on totals from the Social Science Citation Index.

Attaining tenure and a promotion to full professor in 1992 meant I could experiment with new teaching styles without being concerned about risking negative student opinions, which carried much weight at Cal State. My favorite class was, naturally, the capstone advertising class where students submitted a complete advertising proposal for the launch of a real product or service in the pipeline; the work included research, positioning, execution, and evaluation using advertising, sales promotion, public relations, and other communication tools. I was amazed by how smart and creative the students were; they loved to work in groups doing real-life projects. As the years went by, students were finding creative ways to use new technologies in search engines, graphics, media planning, presentation software, and social media, among others.

My students participated in the College World Series of Advertising; an annual national competition sponsored by the American Advertising Federation. The 1995 competition project was an advertising campaign for the launch of the Dodge Neon and presentations took place in the *Los Angeles Times* building with teams from major universities in California, Arizona, and Nevada. My team performed flawlessly and won the top regional award and were off to Tampa, Florida, for the national competition. We took the entire team, including those who were not part of the presentation. In Florida, we experienced disappointment as a paraplegic student who had worked hard with the team got quite sick and had to fly back without being able to see the finals. We ranked in the middle among the 14 teams from around the country. The next day was my birthday, so Sherry and I celebrated in a French restaurant at Disney's Epcot Center. We had Bordeaux wine and had a Napoleon pastry after dinner that reminded of the Napoleon restaurant where I worked almost three decades earlier in Washington DC.

One day when Mike was in the 10th grade of high school, he asked me to go with him to Orange County Superior Court in Santa Ana but did not say why and I didn't ask him. The courthouse was full of high school students there for the Orange County Mock Trial competition. Later, I learned that Mike was a member of the Brea Olinda Mock Trial team that had worked for months with a local attorney on a case involving someone who had been fired from his job for wearing a swastika. The competition was held in the courtroom in front of a sitting judge. Mike was a pre-trial prosecution attorney, and his job was to present the case to the judge. I noticed that most students who made an argument in front of the judge read their parts, but Mike had memorized his entire legal argument and delivered it flawlessly and with confidence. The judge allowed the case to go to trial. I was so proud of him that day and saw something in him that I had never seen. Afterward, the judge made a ruling for the case to go to trial and praised Mike Zandpour for making a compelling presentation. In the car on the way back, I told Mike that I was so impressed with his performance and perhaps he may want to consider pursuing a legal education in college. I figured that may be a good academic goal even if he abandoned the idea down the road.

My parents occasionally visited the United States when they lived in Tehran, but in the early 1990s, they were staying with my brother, Farrokh, in Irvine. We visited them often and sometimes took them to nearby places to show them around. My dad adored his grandchildren and especially enjoyed playing backgammon with Mike. Even into his 90s, my dad liked the slot machines in Vegas and drinking coke. Unfortunately, in January 1994, he had a stroke and passed away a few days later in the Mission Hospital at the age of 96. Fazlullah Zandpour, the man who always loved me, advised me, and protected me was gone! His name, Fazlullah, means the grace and virtue of God. He had chosen Zandpour as his last name during early 1920s when every Iranian citizen was mandated to have a last name. In Farsi, Zandpour means the son of Zand, the name of our ancestral tribe founded by Karim Khan Zand who ruled Iran from 1751 to 1779. Fazlullah was a quiet man, but the day of his funeral was anything but quiet. On January 17, 1994, Southern California was shaken by the 6.7-magnitude Northridge earthquake! My brother, Farhad, aptly mentioned that a true legend wouldn't go quietly. Many friends and families attended the funeral at Rose Hills Memorial Park.

A couple of years after his high school mock trial, Mike was a freshman at Cal State Fullerton University majoring in political science with an eye on becoming a lawyer. It was such a delight to go with Mike to school every day and occasionally run into him on campus. The drawback was that I could no longer share some of the funny family stories with my classes about Mike; he had friends who attended my classes and who told him about my stories but Mike is very private and didn't like it. He was an excellent student and graduated with honors in 1997. In addition to using me as his personal ATM while on campus, he was a founding member of Sigma Phi Epsilon fraternity and worked in a program called Choice 2000 that promoted university education among high school students. Right after graduation, he attended law school at Ohio State University and became a diehard fan of the Buckeyes. He graduated in 2000 and has been working in banking ever since. As of 2024, he is the deputy counsel for City National Bank, but his main job is nourishing and helping to develop my beautiful, athletic, and smart granddaughter, Sophia.

My daughter Melody followed suit and studied criminal justice at Cal State Fullerton, and graduated with honors. She received her law degree from Loyola Law School in Los Angeles California in 2010. In 2024 Melody Zandpour Cox is the regional vice president Pacific Region-Staff Legal at Hartford.

Sherry with Nittany Lion at her graduation at Penn State University when she received her Master of Science in Educational Psychology, 1988.

In my advertising creative class at Cal State University, Fullerton in 1990.

With my nephew Payam in San Diego after completing his term of service at USS BENFORD in 1996.

My nephew Ben's graduation from St. George Medical School at the Lincoln Center in New York in 1998 with my brother Farrokh and our mom.

From left: My youngest brother, Farhad, me, and our cousin and childhood friend Shahram, Washington D.C. area, in early 2000s.

Visiting the University of Hong Kong around 2004 with Professor Ning Ron Liu third from left.

I am leading the College of Communication Processional as the Distinguished Faculty Marshal during the 2009 Commencement Ceremony at Cal State University Fullerton.

From left: My daughter Melody, me and my son, Mike during Melody's California Swearing in Ceremony in 2010 at Loyola Law School in Los Angeles.

CHAPTER 7

Embracing Digital Technology and
International Education

In 1997, I was appointed associate dean of the college of communication. At that time, the college had three departments: communication, speech communications, and radio-TV-film. The department of communication was the most well-known with the largest number of students; it offered popular programs in journalism, advertising, public relations, so on. The speech communications department was the most productive in terms of research and graduate studies; it was split between communication theoretical studies and communicative disorders. The college had an excellent center for children who stuttered that was quite unique and served low-income families for a minimal fee. The department of radio-TV-film was the sole undergraduate program among the three with much focus on film critique and script writing; they hadn't developed programs in directing and producing since the department had no graduate program at that time.

The digital revolution was transforming our world as we approached the new millennium. Some of our instructional content, delivery, and administrative processes were becoming obsolete. Our broadcast journalism students didn't even have access to studio facilities and cameras. Our TV-film faculty members were teaching in a dilapidated analog studio with a 30-year-old audio board. Our communicative disorder faculty were in a speech and hearing clinic that had not been updated for decades. In addition, advances in communication technologies were facilitating rapid growth in international travel and commerce, requiring a workforce for a global economy. Although the college had a few high-profile international scholars, including Stella Ting-Toomey and William Gudykunst, by and large, it was lacking an international orientation. In short, as one of the largest communication programs in the country, it seemed we were rather unprepared to usher in the workforce of the twenty-first century. Other institutions seemed to have similar problems.

I focused my efforts on enhancing technology and international activities at the college in addition to my other responsibilities. Early on, we hired two additional key information technology (IT) support staff, both with graduate degrees in computer science. Another IT staff member was in charge of our Apple graphics labs. There was so much to learn! One of the first books that I read was Bill Gate's *Business @ the Speed of Thought*. I began to attend technology conferences like Comdex and the National Association of Broadcasters (NAB) in Vegas where Apple's Steve Jobs and Microsoft's Bill Gates and other technology leaders were talking about the future of communication. Companies in the forefront of communication technology like Sony and Panasonic were showcasing their amazing new smart products. It felt like our college was in the slow lane of a fast-moving world!

I was shocked to see that journalism and advertising students who were working at *Daily Titan*, the campus newspaper, had no access to computers. I asked Amir Dabirian, a friendly Iranian American who was IT senior manager for help. Amir graciously provided us with the necessary digital equipment and the students showed their appreciation by dedicating one full page of the *Daily Titan* to thank me and Amir. Amir also helped us get our large internship program online to make it more convenient for students to apply and more efficient for the college to assess student performance, recordkeeping, and site monitoring. As technology environment evolved, Amir helped develop new versions of our internship software.

Around the same time, I visited my old college friend, Manny Bahrami, at the Library of Congress where he was a senior electrical engineer. He showed me the Cisco IPTV that could be used for streaming video on our campus network. When the college acquired a new TV Studio, we decided to turn it into a center for production, distribution, and storage of digital video with the mission of creating a practical learning environment for students. We purchased the IPTV system and the Cisco engineers successfully installed it. It was a real coup to run video on the campus network for the first time. We all felt we were at the dawn of an exciting new era; there was no widespread Windows Media Player, no Facebook, and no You-Tube or Instagram yet!

We called the new center Titan Communication after the name of a capstone advertising class I had developed several years earlier where students worked with clients and charged for services in a practical learning environment. Shortly after its creation, a flurry of digital activities began: Lynne Gross, a professor in the department of radio-television-film used the facility to create Titan internet radio and Chancellor Reed of the Cal State University System, President Milton Gordon, and others participated in the ribbon-cutting ceremony. Students loved the internet radio and we soon had more than 70 student DJs who worked there as part of their extracurricular activities. Students created the video magazine *On-the-Edge* under the supervision of one our colleagues, Eraj Shadaram. Professor Tony Fellow, a journalism professor, started a weekly show called *The World Press*, and many others followed over the years. Titan Communication eventually started to live stream graduation ceremonies for family and friends unable to attend the ceremony in person. This was particularly important since most of our graduates were firs-generation college students with large families, and for those who lived far away or resided in foreign countries.

Later in 1999, I was part of a group writing a grant proposal for small business technology transfer when I met Alice Lei, president of Nightingale Technologies. We were both interested in emerging e-commerce communication technologies. My focus was educating faculty and students, and she wanted to help bring the small business community up to speed. We created and co-chaired eight annual Orange County eBusiness Education Conferences that ran from 2000 to 2007. We brought in other partners like the US Small Business Administration, National Women Business Owners, Orange County Transit Authority, a variety of chambers of commerce, Asian Women Entrepreneurs, and a numberer of other partners. We invited successful online entrepreneurs to tell their stories; one was acting as an online wholesale agent for small European chocolatiers and told us how she attracted customers to her site, Chocolate Epicure, by putting all kinds of chocolate recipes and their backstories on her website. Another person had transformed her father's small fishing supply store into a successful online venture, providing how-to techniques and tips, including gears, baits, and tactics for ice fishing; I think it was called BigFishtacle.com. These types of businesses, whether they survived or not, were pioneers in converging the function of advertising, selling, and publishing.

We also organized several educational workshops for the community in collaboration with the Asian Business Association of Orange County including "Surviving Tough Times through Effective Communication" and "Re-launch Your Business." I kept my connection with Alice and participated in her Advisory Board of Asian Women Entrepreneurs of Orange County. There was much excitement in the air as the whole world was rapidly changing, but unfortunately, little enthusiasm among a few of my colleagues who were oblivious how business, science, and education were dramatically being transformed and they were sticking to the old curricula and syllabi.

Sherry was in Iran for the first time in 22 years to attend her niece's wedding and I was still in bed on September 11, 2001, when Melody called and told me to turn on the TV. The first thing I heard on TV was about the evacuation of the White House. It was surreal. A group of Al-Qaeda members who were in Afghanistan with the assistance of the Taliban regime under the leadership of Osama Bin Laden, all from Saudi Arabia, attacked the United States by hijacking and crashing two commercial passenger planes into the Twin Towers of the World Trade Center in New York City. Another plane crashed into the Pentagon and a fourth crashed into an open field near Shanksville, Pennsylvania. About three thousand Americans were killed on that day. I heard universities might be targeted too, so I decided to cancel all communication classes since we were the only academic unit in a 10-story building called College Park. This was an emergency decision out of abundance of caution, albeit without the university president's authorization since he was not available.

The whole nation was in shock; no one had experienced anything like it. There was a cloud of deep sadness, anger, and suspicion in the air. Suddenly, men of Middle Eastern descent were targets of suspicion; anyone wearing a turban or sporting a heavy beard was assumed to be Bin Laden—the mastermind of the attack—or one of his followers and was an immediate a target. The owner of a restaurant close to our building who was an Indian Sikh had replaced his turban and apron with US flags and stood in front of his Indian restaurant waving the US flag in response to numerous threats he had received. Another Sikh man who owned a gas station was mistaken as a Middle Eastern Islamic militant and was killed. Ironically, Sikhs and Muslims are diametrically opposed and often have conflicts in India where there is a large population of both religions.

The entire country was in a state of bewilderment, to put it mildly. Several days later, President Bush delivered a calming address from the Washington National Cathedral to soothe the worries of an anxious nation. Everyone at the university wanted to watch the address so I asked our webmaster to video stream it via our IPTV on the campus network. Apprehensive and fearful, faculty, staff, and students huddled around PC monitors to watch the president's speech. We all needed that moment of reassurance from the president. I thought President Bush stepped up to plate and performed exceptionally well.

Several years later, we hired TV Magic to upgrade two of our studios and create a dedicated studio with robotics for our broadcast journalism program, all housed in Titan Communication. Getting rid of obsolete curriculum and equipment was like pulling teeth. For example, when we wanted to replace cameras that used celluloid film with camcorders to provide hands-on training for many more students or when converting a dilapidated studio with a 35-year-old analog sound board into a modern digital studio, we faced stiff resistance mostly from faculty who seldom taught in TV studios.

As the world became an integrated production and marketing network, I was convinced that we had to prepare our students for a global economy. One of my most productive international education initiative was the creation of the Communications Master of Arts program in Hong Kong in collaboration with the University of Hong Kong School of Professional and Continuing Education (HKU Space). The program made it possible for several of our faculty to teach professional students in Hong Kong, an international business and trade hub.

Early in 2000, Professor Ning Liu from HKU Space sent me a letter about a possible partnership with our college. They had an innovative model of partnering with a variety of universities and prestigious programs, such as The London School of Economics, but ours would be their first partnership with a US university. I was excited about the opportunity of working with the University of Hong Kong as it was among the most prestigious in Asia. In addition, the potential partnership was the first of its kind at Cal State University. It was a lucky moment when our preparation and enthusiasm intersected with a wonderful opportunity! There was no doubt in my mind that teaching in the Hong Kong setting would enrich the faculty experience and, in turn, that of our students. I started to float the idea around, seeking faculty support. A few colleagues were against the potential partnership; their main objective was that we shouldn't be helping the Chinese!

We managed to get enough administrative and faculty support to explore the possibilities. I had ideas for how the program might work. It had to be financially sustainable and in line with the policies of the Western Association of Colleges and Universities (WASC), the accrediting agency for the university. As a first step, we invited professor Enoch Young, HKU Space director, and professors Shen Shir-Ming and Ning Liu to visit Cal State Fullerton. They accepted our invitation and we had a discussion as to how we could proceed. The faculty was still kind of lukewarm about the idea, but I was determined to push it forward. Before we went to Hong Kong, I put together a preliminary memorandum of understanding (MOU) between the two institutions and ran it by the folks involved.

Around July of 2000, Dean Rick Pullen and I visited Hong Kong for the first time and stayed in the Island Pacific Hotel where our faculty would stay while teaching in Hong Kong. It was a comfortable hotel and our rooms had the perfect view of Victoria Harbor. The night view of Hong Kong's skyline was just amazing. We arrived in Hong Kong in the early evening, but the next morning, Hong Kong Observatory issued a warning for a tropical cyclone or typhoon that required a lockdown. People of Hong Kong take typhoon warnings seriously since one killed about ten thousand people in early 1900. Fortunately, around the evening time, there was an all-clear signal and we visited the HKU Space office and got the (MOU) signed.

The day after signing the MOU, we all went to Shanghai where HKU Space was planning to offer the MA program. I was quite impressed by their many modern skyscrapers; China seemed much more advanced than I had imagined. The market economy was in full swing thanks to Deng Xiaoping's vision and reforms about 20 years earlier. The country was enjoying an average annual growth of about 10 percent. A Chinese educator said, "the giant dragon is finally awake!"

I was invited to give a presentation about the role of the internet in business and education at their learning center. The conference room was on one of the top floors of a tall modern building with large windows all around it and the view was amazing. I started by saying that the audience should be proud of their country. All they needed to do was look at the magnificent buildings around us. The room erupted in applause, appreciating my acknowledgment of their country's success. I went on and told them that the internet was turning the 4Ps of marketing upside down and the business wouldn't be usual anymore! Products were customized, prices were fluid, promotion was interactive, and place of sales were everywhere, which was still news to a lot of people in 2000. That evening, HKU Space organized a reception with potential students in a private room at a restaurant. There were about 10 round tables in the room, but unlike Americans who normally have individual conversations around each table, the entire room was engaged in a collective light and friendly conversation, exchanging jokes and funny stories. We all had a great time. Afterward, we went to the Bund and walked on the bank of the Huangpu River.

After a couple of days, my counterpart Dr. Ning Lui took us to Beijing—my first time there. One of the first places we visited was the Great Wall, and it is truly an amazing manmade structure. I felt the Wall represented the Chinese culture of determination, hard work, and long-term orientation. The wall integrated the functions of defense, transportation, and communication and I learned that construction started as early as 220 BCE by Qin Shi Huang and was updated in the following centuries, including the addition of the watchtowers that were built by the founder of the Ming Dynasty. Beyond blocking enemies, the wall was used to transport soldiers and materiel during battle; successive watchtowers were used to alert troops about invading armies by sending messages through smoke and fire.

When we returned to Fullerton, I started to work on the program. We planned it as a mixed model of online and face-to-face meetings. Students had a few weeks of online contact to become acquainted with their readings and other preparations, followed by two weeks of intensive face-to-face lectures during the intersessions and summers in Hong Kong. Finally, students had a few weeks of research and writing with online access to faculty after they returned to Fullerton. Our university owned the degree, so we took responsibility for the curriculum, providing the faculty and conducting student evaluation, whereas HKU Space was responsible for recruiting students, classroom rental, collecting tuition and paying faculty salaries. I worked closely with the interested faculty and the university administrators to develop the curriculum and business plan as well as securing WASC's substantive change approval. WASC wanted a detailed plan and an oral presentation with Q&A. We were successful and managed to bypass the dean of university extended education's strong opposition! According to our plan, faculty were to receive funding for airfare and hotel costs in addition to a $5,000. stipend for two weeks' work.

Shortly after the start of the program in early 2003, SARS (severe acute respiratory syndrome) reached Hong Kong; the Center for Disease Control (CDC) issued a travel advisory and restricted travel to Hong Kong. As a result, except for Professor Cindy King who was brave enough to tough it out, all other faculty members scheduled to teach in Hong Kong refused to travel. Without our faculty in Hong Kong, the program was in jeopardy. Fortunately, we managed to use our Titan Communications facility to stream the lectures to Hong Kong classrooms, which was quite innovative at the time.

In May of 2004, we had our first joint commencement ceremony. Our president and a few top administrators from our campus were going to attend. I had to be in Hong Kong a day early to help coordinate with Dr. Ning Liu our very first commencement in a foreign land. I was scheduled to fly with Japan Airlines with an overnight stay in Osaka, Japan. My flight was around 10 a.m. and we were running a bit late so I grabbed my passport from the drawer where I always kept it and Sherry dropped me off at LAX about 45 minutes later.

Finally, when I was at the front of the check-in line but before handing my American passport to the clerk, I decided to look inside. To my great shock, I saw Sherry's picture! In my haste, I had grabbed the wrong passport. After our last trip, I placed Sherry's passport in the same drawer where I kept mine. Somehow, her beautiful smile in the picture had a calming effect on me during that disastrous moment. Fortunately, a Japan Airlines supervisor changed my reservation so that I could fly directly to Hong Kong the next day without being late. She saved my life!

I got to Hong Kong on time and went over the details and speeches with Dr. Lui. The graduation ceremony in Hong Kong was similar to ours, albeit much smaller and without our usual pomp and circumstance. It was great to see the first crop of our communication students receiving their US graduate degrees without taking a single course on our US campus. I thought it was a wonderful model to export our education. However, we did have a few glitches. President Gordon had forgotten to bring his regalia so he borrowed one from the University of Hong Kong that looked nicer than ours. I had taken a US flag with me to display during the ceremony as had been our practice in the US, but it was not permitted without any explanation.

After the commencement, I stayed in Hong Kong for another two weeks to teach. It was customary in Hong Kong that after the last class of the intense two-week session, students invited instructors to a restaurant for dinner or lunch. Students took me to a restaurant where they served burgers with small paper US flags stuck into the buns. As soon as the burgers were served, a few students took out their cigarette lighters and were about to burn the US paper flags. I thought it might be protesting the US invasion of Iraq, and as an American, I was offended so I immediately got up to leave when they stopped. In the decade that I traveled to Hong Kong, I observed it gradually became more Chinese and less British. Many taxicab drivers spoke only Chinese and in general, the social status of the mainland Chinese improved quite a bit. A case in point: When I was in Hong Kong in January of 2012, Dolce & Gabbana was enforcing its policy of banning Hong Kong residents from taking photos inside or outside of its flagship store while allowing those from the mainland to do so. Apparently, the people of Hong Kong had always felt superior to the people of Southeast Asia. After an incident of such discrimination, there was a riot in front of the store and the people of Hong Kong who saw the ban as an insult forced the store to apologize, reverse the policy, and drop the photography ban for Hong Kong residents.

After I left my position as associate dean, I still administered the program until it ended around 2012. It was a unique program in the Cal State system and lasted more than a decade; it paid for itself and brought in some profit for the university. A dozen faculty members taught there repeatedly and loved the experience. I traveled and taught at least once every year; we exported our education and managed to graduate more than 100 students—some of whom I follow on LinkedIn—and are all successful professionals inside and outside of Hong Kong.

In 2004, the Singapore Polytechnic School of Business invited me to serve as their external examiner for a two-year term. I traveled with Sherry to Singapore, stayed there for about two weeks, and prepared a report that I shared with the president of the institution during a meeting. I had been to Singapore in the 1970s when my agency was handling the advertising of Singapore Airlines in collaboration with their agency of record, Singapore Batey. At that time, Singapore seemed underdeveloped and they had just built the Mandarin Hotel. This time, I was totally surprised by the progress they had made. There was a row of luxury hotels, top restaurants, and fine buildings, not to mention their very efficient public transportation system, including their subway. The three ethnic groups: Malays, Chinese, and Indians seemed to live in harmony under the protection of the government. We were there in November during the Muslim New Year celebrations when Malay men, women, and children wore colorful, traditional dresses in public. Women were much more visible in society and professions than three decades ago. The People's Action Party was still in power after all those years. While I was working at the Polytechnic during our stay, Sherry was discovering all the wonderful one-of-a-kind things that Singapore is famous for, such as a collection of exotic birds and a garden of beautiful flowers, among other attractions. We both spent time at Sentosa Island, a beautiful place. I hear it has since been developed into a major resort and casino.

I returned to Singapore as part of my external examiner duties in 2006. Unlike our faculty meetings in the US, theirs were very quiet and faculty members mostly listened to the chair without contributing much, which I thought was a sign of respect for authority. An interesting idea I saw in Singapore Polytechnique was when business students were given a blank sheet of paper to draw a new product of their imagination. Later during subsequent classes, they wrote a plan for production, marketing sales, advertising, and so on. During our meeting, the president told me that there were many "silos" not in communication with one another and that they needed "tunnels" between them to be connected. It was true of Cal State University Fullerton as well—

each college was treated as a silo and much-needed hybrid and interdisciplinary studies were hard to develop. For example, we received a grant, spent a couple of years, and engaged a few marketing and advertising professors to develop a state-of-the-art program in integrated marketing communications, but it died in the curriculum committee due to a disagreement among deans who had no appetite to jointly take a risk and share resources. This was despite the fact that an interdisciplinary program in communication and marketing was an absolute must, due to emerging online stores and e-commerce among other developments. One of our partner universities abroad quickly adopted the program with great success in China.

We had a relationship with Jin-ai University, a private Buddhist educational group that owned kindergartens, elementary schools, high schools, and colleges in the Fukui Prefecture in Japan. In 2004, we were invited to visit Jin-ai University. Our dean brought his wife and I took Sherry.

I had been to Japan when my agency was handling Japan Airlines advertising in Iran, but this was Sherry's first trip. During our first night there, they held a lavish party, reminding me of the warm Japanese hospitality I had experienced in the 1970s. None of the Japanese men had brought their wives and the party started quietly, but after much eating and sake drinking, it became loud with laughter and Japanese conversation.

The next day, the students prepared an entertainment program for us. I was impressed by the talent the students demonstrated in playing instruments, singing, dancing, and gymnastics. They were all so polite and gracious. We gave a presentation about studying in America. One of the professors there was a priest who invited us to an old Buddhist temple in Kyoto, the capital of Japan for more than a thousand years, until the mid-nineteenth century. We participated in the tea ceremony ritual, a spiritual exercise in purifying the soul and a chance to reflect and reset it. In Nara, another ancient city, quite a few people wanted to take pictures with Sherry. To them, her blond hair represented a true American lady! We also visited an old paper mill in Fukui where they were producing handmade paper like they did in the old days. The Japanese love to preserve their history and traditions.

*****

In 2006, I got an invitation from Professor Kim Sanghook to visit Inha University in Seoul, South Korea. I also wanted to visit my classmate from the University of Washington days, Kim Hak-Soo, who was the dean of the communication school at Sogang University. I arrived in Seoul in the late evening and the first thing that caught my eye was how the illumination of their skyline seemed subdued compared with more dazzling nightlights of Hong Kong and Singapore, and I thought perhaps it was a sign of Korean frugality. The Han River that runs through Seoul was magnificent but the relationship between South and North Korea was quite tense and I was a bit hesitant to accept Kim's invitation to give a talk about improving communication skills at the Korean Atomic Energy Research Institute in Daejeon about 100 miles from Seoul. Kim and I traveled by train for about two hours and it was a great opportunity to see the Korea's beautiful countryside. Kim pointed out quite a few cemeteries along the way and told me most families in

Korea have their own private cemetery. As a family's financial situation improved, they would buy land closer to the city so it would be easier to visit their ancestors. My talk at the institute went well and afterward, we were treated to an amazing, authentic Korean lunch on a traditional low table. They also gave me an honorarium in cash besides numerous skin care and personal care products.

The next day, I met the vice president of Inha University and discussed the differences between our two universities. I was surprised by the large number of Korean students who were studying advertising. Professor Sanghook arranged for me to conduct a communication workshop for employees at Daewoo Construction Company, one of the largest companies in Korea. They were involved in making nuclear plants, among other things around the world, and had constructed the track beds for the Tehran-Bandar Abbas railway.

During my last years as an Administrator, I was trying to strengthen our existing international relationships and find new ones for potential future partnerships in terms of student and faculty exchange, and perhaps joint degree programs. In the mid-2000s, Dr. Shen Shir-Ming, the deputy director of HKU Space and head of the Statistical Society in Hong Kong, invited me to present a paper at the seventh International Conference for Statistical Education in Brazil. I welcomed the opportunity to visit the South American country. My colleague professor Tony Rimmer was originally a journalist from New Zealand and agreed to work with me on a paper dealing with the importance of journalism students learning statistics in our increasingly data-driven world.

I had never been to Brazil and was excited about the trip. I managed to convince both of my children, who were single at the time, to go with me and Sherry. We booked our flights with Varig Airlines, Brazil's oldest airline. About a week before our flight, Varig Airline declared bankruptcy and its planes at LAX were confiscated. Mike and Melody immediately canceled their tickets and got refunds through their American Express credit cards but I managed to get replacement tickets. Sherry and I flew first class to Rio de Janeiro with another airline without paying anything extra but I was surprised by how lax airline security was in Brazil.

The conference was in the city of Salvador in the state of Bahia, located on the Atlantic Coast. Salvador seemed more like an African city to me, primarily because the Portuguese Colonial Empire had relied heavily on African slaves for their sugarcane plantations in the seventeenth century.

In our session at the conference, we discussed the significance of an informed citizenry for democracy's survival in the age of information. We got a standing ovation, but our discussion was not relevant to Salvador where, sadly, we saw armies of children begging during school hours and beyond. One evening, we invited Rimmer, Shirming, and their spouses to dinner. During our short walk from where our taxi dropped us off to the entrance of the restaurant, we were stopped at least five times by children with heartbreaking stories and an immediate need for money. Sherry gave them all the Brazilian reals she had. I ran into quite a few dissident students at the conference who complained about the high inflation and corruption in Brazil.

The restaurant was an old brick building with no elevator and our table was on the third floor at the edge of a balcony with almost no railing. It was frightening to think that someone could fall to the courtyard below after a drink or two, and we changed tables. When I went to wash my hands, there was no soap; I kept asking for soap, but they didn't understand me. Sherry eventually came and asked me why I was taking so long. I told her in Farsi that I needed *sabon* (soap) and then they quickly brought us soap; apparently, soap is the same word in Portuguese, the language of Brazil.

We saw children playing soccer everywhere in the streets, reminding me of my childhood. Sherry and I watched the 2006 World Cup Final between France and Italy in the hotel bar. The bar was very crowded and Brazilians mostly rooted for Italy. The teams were tied 1–1 and the winner was decided by penalty kicks, which Italy won 5–3. The bar was electrified and everyone was ecstatic.

In May 2007, I chaired a panel in a conference on international communications that was held in Marathon, Greece. I love Greek food and music and Sherry and I visited Acropolis again, reminding me of my visit to Greece during the Juntas in 1969. The Greeks and Persians were two great ancient civilizations determined to destroy each other. Of course, one of the places the Athenian army defeated the invading Persians around 490 BC—despite being outnumbered—was in Marathon. So, when our tour guide was telling the story of the Greeks stopping the barbarians from reaching Athens, everyone was feeling victorious, except Sherry and me, of course. The idea of Marathon was based on the legend of an ancient Greek messenger who ran from Marathon to Athens for about 26 miles with the news of the Greek victory over Persians.

We stayed at Club Med, quite a nice place, until an army of English Liverpool soccer fans showed up to attend the 2006–2007 UEFA Championship game with Milan, Italy. They all stayed up late and were singing soccer and patriotic victory songs while drinking heavily. The next morning, they all went to Athens Olympic Stadium to cheer the Liverpool team. Unfortunately, Liverpool lost to Milan and when the fans returned to Club Med, they looked like a defeated army and void of their high spirits of the previous night. Many were drunk and violent; they broke things and vomited everywhere. We were relieved when they left the next morning.

With respect to international activities, we had built good relationships with several Asian universities, but had little connection with Europe. I viewed Europe as the birthplace of freedom and democracy so I was excited when my colleague professor Anthony Fellow, who is of Italian descent, suggested that we create a college-based study-abroad program in Florence, Italy. He loved Italy, and I thought it would be a wonderful experience for our students. I facilitated the creation of the program, modeling after our Hong Kong model with a mix of online and face-to-face of instruction. Students would spend part of the program at Fullerton and the rest in Florence to cut down the cost. In addition, we identified a few required courses for graduation that students could substitute with what was taught in Florence. That made the program accessible to many of our first-generation students since they could pay their Cal State University tuition but attend classes in Florence. We hired a company called AFIS to arrange student and faculty air travel as well as classroom and student housing in Florence.

Students were loaned light digital camcorders to film their experiences in Italy and share them on the program website. The program was a smashing success and lasted for about a decade. I had never traveled to Florence and wanted to get the feel of the city and see how our students were doing, besides taking in masterpieces of Renaissance art and architecture. Around 2007, Sherry and I traveled to Barcelona, Rome, Florence, and Venice. In Barcelona, once again, I was reminded of the power of religion when we visited the amazing Basilica Familia Sagrada, a large neo-Gothic Roman Catholic church that had begun in 1740 and was still under construction. It was the work of the famous Catalan architect Antoni Gaudi who died in 1926 in Barcelona. Gaudi's signature is on many important buildings and gardens in Barcelona. Inside the Basilica, you felt the glory of God as was perceived, I suppose, in medieval Europe.

After Barcelona, we went to Rome. This was my second trip to Rome. We saw the Pantheon, a Roman-style temple that originally opened in 125 AD. We also went to see the Colosseum where a lot of hand-to-hand fights were held between gladiators and, sometimes, between gladiators and animals for the entertainment of the Roman emperors and others. The two places were a testament to contrasting human drives: seeking peace and redemption through worship in the Pantheon as opposed to entertainment and gratification through violence in the Colosseum.

We took the train in August 2007 to Florence, the capital of Italy's Tuscany region. Our Florence classes were in session and we met with our students who were hard at work soaking in the rich culture. We visited the Uffizi Gallery adjacent to Piazza Della Signoria in the historic center of Florence. The collection from the period of Italian Renaissance was amazing and showed the massive cultural transformation at the time; we recognized early giant steps toward freedom and democracy. We visited Giotto's bell tower, called the masterpiece of Gothic architecture, located in the Piazza del Duomo as part of Santa Maria Cathedral. As we were walking up, the tower seemed to be going all the way of the heavens! Tony Fellow took us to a Tuscany winery tour where the scenery was breathtaking. Many small and large castles were converted into wineries, each with its own story of Medici and other conspiracies and even murders that happened in the basements of their castles. We visited Chianti winery and drank my favorite wine—it taught us not to ever buy cheap chemical wines!

After our Florence visit, we went to Venice where the streets are canals and you need to take a water taxi to get around. We got out a couple of stops before we were supposed to and had to carry our luggage over the cobblestone alleys. We also visited the famous San Marco Square. That year, we had seen its two replicas: one in the Venetian Resorts in Macau, China, and a more elaborate one in the Venetian resort in Las Vegas.

Right about the time that I left my position as the associate dean of the College of Communications in 2008, I was honored by the United States Small Business Administration (US SBA) for my service to the business community and received the US SBA award at a large reception. I was so happy to share the celebration with Sherry and my mon. As part of that, I received many certificates of achievements including a congratulating certificate from President George W. Bush, California Senator Dianne Feinstein, several congressional recognitions, a California Senate Resolution, a few California Assembly commendations, together with certificate of recognition from the cities of Fullerton, Anaheim, and the County of Orange for my decade-plus of educational service to the business community. It was a nice ending to my administrative work!

In June 2009, Melody's future husband, Brian Cox, invited Sherry and me to dinner at Darya, a nice Persian restaurant in the city of Orange, not too far away from our house in Anaheim Hills. I had met Brian in Big Bear Lake during a ski season. Brian ordered a bottle of Shiraz, a popular red wine named after the city of Shiraz in Iran. Shiraz was home to Saadi and Hafez, great Persian poets of the thirteenth and fourteenth centuries, both of whom wrote many beautiful poems full of wisdom with frequent references to wine and love. After dinner, Brian told us that he wanted to marry Melody if it was okay with us. He seemed like a decent man and I fully trusted Melody's judgment. I particularly liked the fact that he was following our custom of asking the parents for permission. I told him if Melody loved him and wanted to marry him, it was fine with us, and that Iranians always want an appropriate wedding ceremony and reception for their daughters, and we would like to share the cost.

Brian and Melody had a magnificent wedding reception with about three hundred guests. His uncle Simon Tavassoli hired a famous Iranian pianist. Our friend from church Joe Landi and a scientist friend Dr. Bahram Kermani conducted the ceremonies in line with Christian and Persian cultural traditions. A Persian band played both Western and Iranian songs, we had an open bar, and the dinner was catered by Hatam Restaurant. It was a wonderful night. My friends Manny and his wife, other friends, and our cousins from the East Coast also attend the wedding. In the following years, Brian and Melody gave us three sweet boys—Elliott, Brandon, and Benjamin in 2012, 2014, and 2016 respectively. Since they married, Melody and Brain have lived close to our home; Sherry and I are blessed to frequently spend time with the boys.

Around 2011, HKU Space invited me to conduct a workshop in Guangzhou in mainland China about the impact of internet technology on television. Sherry and two assistants, Ada and Cindy, accompanied me. We took a train from Hong Kong to Guangzhou, which took about two hours. Guangzhou is a huge city with a population of about 15 million people. As soon as we arrived, I was taken aback by the heavy air pollution I could feel in my nose. We had heard businessmen from around the world go there and buy the stuff to import into their countries. Sherry's cousin Khosro, who had a shoe factory in Iran, told us that it was much more profitable to import from Guangzhou than to manufacture it in Tehran and deal with labor issues and supply shortages. He closed his manufacturing plant and imported from China instead.

The workshop lasted about three days and I was quite impressed by the knowledge of the participants about the media in the United States. A lady had a magazine for corporate presidents and I noticed all the pictures in her magazine were long shots and in groups. A gentleman who was the publisher of a glossy food magazine shared the latest issue with the class that was full of great photography but did not show a single picture of a person. Perhaps both businesspeople reflected the collective nature of Chinese culture that places less emphasis on the individual than does the US, which shows individuals up close and personal. The 20-hour seminar went well, and I learned quite a bit from the participants. One of the main issues of discussion was a lack of collaboration and accurate communication between central and local governments that was partly due to growing pains of a giant country leapfrogging to the future. When it was time for the final project, all insisted on doing it as a group instead of individually. I found the students professional, talented, and quite informed about American communication issues and the challenges we were all embracing in the age of media convergence as broadcasters were doing print and print media were using motion pictures.

In 2011, I was invited together with a group of my university colleagues to visit Turkey as part of an outreach effort to American academics. I was experiencing a variety of emotions as we boarded our Turkish Airline flight to Istanbul—I was going to be closer to Iran than I had been since leaving it more than three decades earlier. Our event leader, Tezcan Inanlar, also traveled with us. Turkey shares more than three hundred miles of border with Iran and Turks are the largest ethnic minority in Iran. I began to pull my Iranian-Turkish childhood friends, classmates, and business associates from the depth of my memory.

Turkey and Iran were archrivals, especially during sixteenth to eighteenth centuries when Turkey was part of the Ottoman Empire and the Safavid dynasty ruled Iran from the fifteenth to eighteenth centuries. The two kingdoms engaged in several wars that resulted in the Ottoman's victory and Iran's loss of

Mesopotamia and its other regions. Interestingly, most dynasties that ruled Iran during the last thousand years were Turkish, including Safavid and Qajar. After WWI, Turkey and Iran had parallel political developments. Reza Shah and Ataturk were military officers who became the leaders of Iran and Turkey, respectively, in 1920s, several years after the end of the war. They both worked hard to establish secular governments and modernize their countries. Reza Shah was the founder of the Pahlavi dynasty and continued in the Iranian tradition of monarchical rule as a king; Ataturk founded the Republic of Turkey and became Turkey's president.

This was my second trip to Turkey since my 1969 visit. We arrived in Istanbul in the early evening and our host took us straight to a traditional Turkish restaurant where they served kebobs, rice, and Turkish bread, but unfortunately, none of the Americans could figure out how to use the Turkish traditional restroom. In Istanbul, we stayed in an apartment on top of a girl's school where, from a loudspeaker of a nearby mosque, we heard the *adhan* every morning, the Islamic call to prayer. Istanbul is a magnificent city where the Bosporus Strait waterway divides the Asian and European sides of the city.

I was so impressed by the airports, airlines, freeways, hotels in Turkey that had a vibrant economy with great infrastructure. We met many Turkish people, attended dinner parties, and stayed overnight at the home of a university professor and his pharmacist wife who covered her hair in line with the Islamic hijab. Sunni Islam is the major religion in Turkey as opposed to Shia Islam in Iran. Most people were religious, although two assistants at our hostess' pharmacy were wearing short skirts and makeup without hijabs. It seemed in Turkey that women had a choice of whether to wear a hijab. This was like the old Iran during the shah, but Islamic Republic laws made it illegal for women to be in public places without a hijab. The hijab seems to have become a political and religious pillar of the Islamic Republic of Iran. Quite a few women in our family in Iran were mistreated, assaulted, and even flogged for just showing their hair. The totalitarian regime of Iran has spent much money and human resources on enforcing the hijab, a rule that has caused much pain and suffering, especially among younger generations who tend to resist it at all costs.

As part of our program, we visited the Jewish Rabbinate's office in Istanbul and talked to a spokesperson. She complained about the dwindling Jewish population in Turkey, attributing the decline primarily to being harassed and mistreated. She mentioned that, for example, after any news about Israeli-Palestinian aggressions, Turkish Jewish children become targets of hatred and beatings at school.

We met with the president of Turkish Radio and Television (TIR) who was unhappy about the American invasion of Iraq under President Bush. One of our colleagues asked him about Turkey's human rights efforts. He responded in Turkish, and while the translator was struggling to find the right words in English, I saw that Farsi shared words with Arabic roots and told my colleagues that the gentleman was saying that Turkey was all about respecting human dignity. Everyone was impressed with my Turkish language skills, of which I had none, but I let it go. The same evening, the second in command of TIR, who spoke English, invited our small group to tea and baklava. He approached me and tactfully asked how I learned Turkish. I told him that Farsi and Turkish share many Arabic words because of both countries' long tradition of Islam. We both laughed when I told him I spoke no Turkish.

We were visiting the Blue Mosque with bright blue tiles, the Ottoman legacy of seventeenth-century architecture, when my friend Tony Fellow asked me if I could translate a line in Arabic written on the top of a wall: *Bismillah Rahman Rahim*. It something I heard frequently while growing up. It means "in the name of God, the merciful and compassionate." They were all surprised that I spoke Arabic, but my claim to fame was quite short when I told them that these words are common in Farsi and everyone was familiar with their meaning. Tezcan's Turkish contact who was showing us the mosque said that as an Iranian, I should go back to Iran. He wasn't used to a diverse society and didn't think the ethnic Kurds could call themselves Turks. He was confusing Turk ethnicity with being a citizen of Turkey. He believed ethnicity and nationality were inseparable and told us about an Asian man who had said he was American despite not looking American at all. I told him in America, race is not tied to citizenship, at least not now!

We also visited *Zaman*, a major Turkish newspaper, and met with the chief editor. One of my colleagues asked him why Turkey keeps people in jail for a long time before they can see a judge. The answer was that Turkey was short of judges! At Kanal Turk TV, we met with top management and saw the taping of an entertainment program. We heard that after the 2015 coup in Turkey, police had stormed their offices for corruption and other reasons, including criticism of the ruling justice and development party. Sherry and I were excited to visit Topkapi Palace, since we had seen the very popular and long series, *Suleiman the Magnificent*, featuring the Ottoman king who lived there with his many wives and children, but it was turned in a museum. The museum curator greeted us and told us how various sultans of the Ottoman Empire used the palace and where the formal ceremonies took place. Sherry became quite unhappy when the curator talked about how women kept in the palace had to watch events from a hole upstairs without being seen. The curator was defending the old practice, so I diplomatically changed the subject to the beautiful architecture of the palace.

Hagia Sophia is a magnificent building that was designed and built by the Greeks in sixth century AD. It changed hands from the Christian Roman Empire to Byzantine Easter Orthodox Church, briefly was a Latin Catholic cathedral, and after the Ottoman Turks conquered Constantinople from the Byzantine Empire, they made it a mosque until the dissolution of Ottoman Empire after World War I and the Turkish War of Independence and the creation of the Republic of Turkey. Mustafa Kemal Ataturk, the founder of modern Turkey, converted it to a museum around 1935.

Among the most interesting places we visited was Konya where Jalal al-Din Mohammad Rumi, a thirteenth-century Persian poet and Sufi mystic, taught and was buried. Rumi was born to native Farsi-speaking parents in Balkh about a thousand years ago, during the Khwarazmi Empire. He lived most of his life in Turkey and wrote many, if not all, his great poetry in Farsi but they have been translated to major languages around the world. While visiting the Rumi Museum, Sherry was concerned that despite of all the poems on the walls being in Farsi, they pretended that Rumi was Turkish since there was no mention of Iran or Persia. Later, we visited Rumi University in Konya and learned about Turkey's strategy of gaining soft power influence in the region by building schools, hospitals, and developing academic ties in the Turkic-speaking central Asian countries like Kazakhstan, Turkmenistan, and Uzbekistan.

In Antalya, Turkey, we had a dinner of freshly caught trout and oven-fresh bread in a casual café by a gorgeous river; the setting reminded me of Iran. In Kayseri, a large industrial town, we met a group of young entrepreneurs and people were so proud of their economic progress and eager to show it off to us Americans. There seemed to be consensus that Turkey had no need to join the European Union because it enjoyed economic success. Among the most interesting places we visited was in Cappadocia; a cone-shaped rock formation and a Bronze-age home carved into valley walls that had been later used by Christians.

Early in January 2012, when we got back from Turkey, I was having lunch in our cafeteria with a few friends when the president of the university approached our table and anxiously asked if we knew someone who could speak Afghani. He was with a group of three educators from Afghanistan who were visiting our university as part of the state department's outreach. I didn't believe there was a language called Afghani, but I knew people in Afghanistan spoke Pashto and Dari among other languages. I noticed the women were speaking Dari, which is similar to Farsi, so I told the president that I could translate. Everybody was amazed by how many languages I could speak although I told them the truth. But the ladies were saying that Afghanistan was primarily a tribal and ultrareligious society so most men thought like the Taliban and opposed education for women. They added that some men threw acid in the face of female teachers and students on their way to school, and at night, they burned girls' schools. It was so sad to hear their stories.

I visited Barcelona, shortly after Spain's victory over Italy winning UEFA Euro 2012. I congratulated the taxicab driver for the country winning the European soccer championship. He did not have much of a reaction, except he told me yes, they won, but they didn't acknowledge the presence of five Catalans in the team. When I mentioned that exchange to a professor from Barcelona, he was not surprised and told me they were working on a referendum and wanted autonomy for Catalan. He said that most people in Catalan, where Barcelona is located, feel that Spain was taking their resources and was not giving anything in return. It was the first time that I heard about the rift between Madrid and Barcelona.

I was there to present a paper at the social exchange conference about the implication of national cultures on Facebook users in terms of self-disclosure, friendship, and celebrity fandom. During the trip, I visited the school of journalism at Abat Oliba, CEU, to pitch my idea of developing a joint program for food and wine that involved journalism, advertising, and public relations. The idea was for US students to spend time in Spain and Spanish students to spend time in America. Unfortunately, Spain soon faced an economic downturn and our project was placed on the back burner. As it was our second time in Barcelona, Sherry and I managed to navigate the Barcelona subway and take the train to Montserrat, a peaceful place in the mountains to see the magnificent Montserrat abbey.

When we returned, I continued my research exploring national cultural patterns reflected on television and social media. But this time, I decided to conduct a comparative study of national cultures by looking at the annual speeches of heads of states in the General Assembly at the United Nations. If there were differences in patterns of communications, we should be able to see them by looking at UN speeches. We also learned of an interesting theoretical framework in Richard Nisbett's book *The Geography of Thought: How Asians and Westerners Think Differently*. Nisbett was at Stanford at the time and probably one of the top scholars in culture and cognition studies in America. His theory resonated with what I had personally experienced living in two cultures, making a distinction between "systematic thinking" and "holistic thinking." We collected our data by asking the United Nation Dag Hammarskjold Library to send us 10 years' worth of speeches given by leaders of countries around the world that had been translated into English by UN personnel. Students loved the project and worked tirelessly and eagerly for months on the content analysis of the speeches as part of their research.

During my last year as a full-time professor in 2014 and just before my retirement, five of the graduate students developed a paper and presentation based on the findings titled, "A Decade of United Nation's Speeches by World Leaders" and entered it into the journalism week contest held at the University of Abat Oliba, CEU, Barcelona, Spain. Entries from students from all over Europe were received, and our project was accepted for a presentation. I managed to get a small scholarship for each of my students to take them to Barcelona.

In Barcelona, my students gave an impressive presentation and made our university proud in terms of the content and delivery. I enjoyed watching the presentations of intellectually advanced European students and comparing notes about communication education in the United States and Europe. During the meetings, there was a lot of discussion about Catalan's autonomy and an upcoming referendum. There were discussions about the British exit from the European Union, the Basque separatists, the Flemish in Belgium, and quite a few other places! I wondered about the underlying political, social, and economic causes of such intense desire for national and ethnic autonomy around the world.

One evening, I went to my favorite place in Barcelona, Catalan Cerveceria. I loved their tapa, small savory Spanish dishes. I took a chair at the bar next to two older Catalan businessmen. They had ordered something that looked interesting so I asked them what it was, but without telling me, they ordered it for me. When they found out I was an American professor, they opened up about the politics of Spain and Catalan; we had a long conversation about their desire to separate from Spain— the Spanish government forced students to learn Spanish in Barcelona schools but did not require students to learn Catalan in Madrid and other places. They also told me Barcelona was quite productive and the government was taxing them heavily but was not returning resources to Catalonia. They were both passionate about their beliefs. At the end, they did not let me pay and told me I was considered their guest in Barcelona.

*****

I always wanted to visit Russia so in July 2012, Sherry and I took a Holland America Baltic cruise from London to St. Petersburg. It was a wonderful trip. Every morning, we arrived in a new country. The first was Copenhagen, Denmark where Sherry and I had visited the headquarters of my old client, Tuborg Beer Brewery, during an international advertising Agency Association conference in the 1970s when we were living in Iran. So, the first thing we did was go to a sidewalk café and order a Tuborg beer; the fresh lager tasted good and reminded me of my youth and advertising in Iran!

In Stockholm, Sweden, we saw the great Vasa ship in the Vasa Museum. We were told the ship was the symbol of Sweden imperial days. It sank on its maiden voyage due to poor planning, lack of proper balance, and heavy guns and ornaments in front of horrified onlookers in the early 1600s. Apparently, many knew that the ship wasn't safe, but no one dared to let King Gustav know as he was in a hurry to deploy the ship. I guess there is a lesson there. That is exactly what happens to dictators in closed societies when no one dares to tell them the truth.

The highlight of that trip was beautiful St. Petersburg where we visited the second largest museum in the world, Hermitage Museum. We could spend days looking at the wonderful collections there but we managed to see Raphael's "Madonna and Child" that beautifully showed the love of the Virgin Mary for Jesus. I was curious about the state of religion in Russia in 2012 after decades of godless communist indoctrination efforts. One of the tour guides told me that most Russian politicians pretended to be devout Christians and made sure people knew they regularly attend the Russian Orthodox Church. We also saw some work done by French and Western artists who had escaped the French revolution of 1789.

We saw the magnificent castle of Catherine the Great, the longest-reigning empress of Russia who ruled from 1762 to 1796. She was the daughter of German prince and worked hard to modernize Russia; during her reign, Russia advanced culturally and militarily. Catherine significantly expanded the Russian borders, including bringing an integral part of Iran (Persia) under Russian control, the vast region between the Caspian and Black seas. One of the tour guides told me privately that most Russians were yearning to capture the old Russian glory.

Most places where we went shopping offered vodka, which reminded me of a Russian female student that I had in Hong Kong whose final project was titled something like "Saving the Russian Blood." Her project was an integrated communication campaign against drinking vodka that she thought was contaminating and destroying the blood of Russians.

In November 2013, a former Hong Kong joint program student, Meiying, invited me to visit the Sino-German school in Tianjin about 85 miles from Beijing. Sherry and I took the high-speed train from Beijing to Tianjin; it took us about 30 minutes on the impressive high-speed Chinese train. These trains were everywhere and were as good the European high-speed trains, if not better, and I wondered why we didn't have any in the US. We stayed on campus and the hospitality was great. We spent quite a bit of time with students who were learning to assemble A320 Airbus aircrafts as part of industrial cooperation between China's aviation and Airbus. It was an excellent model of academic–industry collaboration. Sherry had never visited Beijing so we visited the Great Wall together on a very cold day.

Folks at the Sino-German Institute wanted to learn more about the American higher education system and were hoping to develop a student exchange program for graduates. The latter was impossible since they were only a three-year vocational institution and our university did not recognize their degree. For undergraduate transfers, there were additional problems of certification of general education courses. I gave a couple of presentations about our culture of evidence, strategic planning, and operational issues in an academic setting. They suggested that they were already doing strategic planning and were even ahead of the US but based on my private conversations, I knew that was not true. They were about to open a new student center and wanted some input on that, albeit without providing me with any briefing whatsoever.

One evening, the president organized a nice reception in one of the most elegant hotels that I have ever seen. People drank wine like they were drinking brandy or tequila. After a few toasts, the president asked my opinion about the learning center. Without any briefing or visit to the center, I told him that I had no idea. I guess that wasn't a diplomatic response, but it was true. The next day, I had a meeting with the art department faculty and right before going to the meeting, I visited the restroom that looked like hundreds of soldiers had just been there. It was a huge contrast to the night before at the ultra-luxury hotel. During the meeting, I could not help but think that the faculty was okay with the condition of that restroom. I mentioned it to Meiying who agreed that it was not good for the school's brand and told me she would let the president know. I guess I could say the irony was really part of China's growing pains; the West took centuries to reach modernity but China was trying to adopt a modern life in a hurry.

Meiying graciously gave us a tour of Tianjin concessions—territories taken from the Qing dynasty during colonial wars and that were controlled by the colonial powers by the eve of World War II. We saw buildings with diverse European, Japanese, and American architecture that reminded everyone about the China's colonial past. I saw anger and resentment in the eyes of my former student as she pointed to each legacy building.

One of the highlights of the Tianjin trip was a surprise Thanksgiving dinner they had prepared in respect of the American tradition and we celebrated with 20 students from Meiying's class. They had decorated the room with posters of the *Mayflower* and other visuals related to Thanksgiving and prepared a small bird with other food that we all enjoyed together. I presented a little story about the pilgrims, the *Mayflower*, and the harvest celebration. We had a great time.

In 2014, I presented a research paper dealing with self-disclosure, friendship and fandom at the Knowledge, Technology and Society Annual Conference in Madrid, Spain. Findings were based on more than a thousand random users of Facebook and 16 countries individualistic cultures, especially Americans, who had more online friends and were more likely to belong to a celebrity fandom group. The work was published in the *Journal of Technology and Society*. After the conference and my presentation, Sherry and I took the high-speed train to Malaga, Spain, to visit my cousin Moji Karimi who I hadn't seen for at least 30 years. We had stayed connected through LinkedIn. Moji and his daughter Rosalin picked us up from the train station and we had so much to talk about that we spent all day in their restaurant drinking wine and eating pizza. I was happy to hear his son was a doctor practicing in England. We compared note about life in Spain versus the United States. Life in Spain looked a lot more laid back than the US. The economy was depressed and there was much talk about King Carlos, who abdicated the throne that year, and his daughter Infanta Cristina and her husband who were being investigated for corruption. The restaurant business was quite slow but a man sitting outside behind a small table was selling lottery tickets at a brisk pace; I guess for him, the economy was pretty good.

We made another trip to southern Spain in the summer of 2015 with Mike, his wife, Alice, and our lovely six-year-old granddaughter, Sophia. Alice's fluent Spanish made the trip much more enjoyable. I was so happy to be with Sophia on her first trip to Europe. We had a wonderful time in Madrid and took the high-speed train to Barcelona. We went to my favorite place, Cerveceria Catalan for tapas, drank much sangria, and had much fun. In Barcelona, I saw the son of my cousin Mitra, Ali Zandpour, for the first time. Ali, his German wife, and their children were living in Marbella, a beautiful Spanish city by the Mediterranean Sea. Mike and his family took a Disney cruise from Barcelona while Sherry and I took the high-speed train to Paris, France.

When we complained about our hotel room, we lucked out and the clerk gave us a suite on the top floor where we could see the Eiffel Tower from the window of one room and the Seine River from another. The next day, my architect cousin Bahman Pourhamidi came with his Japanese wife, Hitomi, and his daughter, Sayeh, who worked for L'Oreal, on a special tour. We saw the famous Basilica of the Sacred Heart of Paris and had lunch at the oldest restaurant in Paris, Café Procope, which had been frequented by Voltaire and Rousseau as well as many French artists, literary figures, and philosophers, since it opened its doors in 1686. There was so much history in every room of that restaurant. I was delighted to see Bahman; it had been about 40 years since Sherry and I had dinner with him and Hitomi in Paris right before the Islamic Revolution. Bahaman is very smart and, among thousands of applicants, had been accepted to the prestigious medical school at the University of Tehran but my Aunt Giti had bitter experiences from her ex-husband medical doctor and discouraged him. Instead, he went to Paris to become an architect and later became a French citizen. He looked and acted French and had integrated well into the society.

While in Paris, we spent time with Sherry's nieces, Mahsa and Rasta, who were both French citizens teaching at the university level in Paris. They took us on another nice tour, including the famous Café de la Paix across from the Paris Opera building where many well-dressed French were having their afternoon coffee and pastries. They mentioned that there was much discrimination and prejudice in France toward the people of the Middle East and Africa. They said they always put their pictures on their résumés so an employer could see they were not wearing the Islamic hijab. It reminded me of President Regan words in addressing US immigrants: people could live in France or Japan all their lives but could never call themselves French or Japanese, while in the United States, they could say "I am an American" regardless of where they were born. France was extremely segregated and opportunities for upward mobility were quite limited for the poor. Sherry and

I visited the Louvre Museum and saw many pieces of Iranian art and culture, from ancient to modern. In addition, it had an extensive exhibition of the Islamic arts. I wondered how those pieces got out of Iran.

When we returned home, there was a ray of hope about the future of the Iranian people when China, France, Germany, Russia, the United Kingdom, the United States, the European Union, and Iran signed a Joint Comprehensive Plan of Action (JCPOA) ensuring Iran's nuclear activities would be only for peaceful purposes. As a result, some of the severe Western sanctions were removed. It seemed Iran was going to be open for business and foreign investments soon and that Iran was on its way to gradually join the rest of the world in commerce, travel, and education. The Iran nuclear program and her access to atomic weapons had been a hot button for the international community for years. The Iranian government argued that having atomic energy was the country's right but the US and Western allies did not trust the Islamic regime of Iran. As a result, Iran had been put under heavy sanctions called " maximum pressure." The first impact of that was the devaluation of Iranian currency that made imports exorbitantly expensive.

I was hoping the potential partnership with the West would gradually transform the belligerent and uncompromising position of Iran into an attitude conducive to creating a vibrant, innovative, and open modern society by capitalizing on Iranian ingenuity and its rich culture and there were some early hopeful signs. For example, Boeing and Airbus were planning to sell commercial jetliners to Iran to replace aging and unsafe Iran Air planes and the giant French petroleum company, Total, and a few other

Western companies were beginning to work with Iranian companies. Unfortunately, all of that came to a screeching halt in 2018 when President Trump took the United States out of the JCOPA and renewed all the previous severe sanctions.

The renewed isolation of Iran and severe sanctions were counterproductive! The people of Iran suffered tremendously. Iran was pushed firmly into the camp of China and Russia who helped Iran accelerate its unchecked advancement in nuclear, missile, and drone technologies so much so that in 2024, Iran is exporting thousands of drones and missiles to Russia in support of its invasion of Ukraine. In the meantime, Iran has been expanding and strengthening its proxy forces in Yemen, Lebanon, Syria, Iraq, and Gaza with the promise of keeping the US out of the Middle East and ultimately destroying Israel. The architect and coordinator of Iranian-backed militant forces was Qasem Soleimani, an Iranian major general who was killed in Iraq by an American drone strike in early January 2020, opening a new chapter of animosity between Iran and the United States. The clerics seldom refer to the non-cleric Soleimani as "General" Soleimani, I suppose because of their disdain for the formal army and its Western style of rankings. Instead, they refer to him by his first name, Ghasem, adding the title of Haj to his name that signifies his pilgrimage to Mecca, the holiest place in Islam, thereby portraying him as a Muslim icon and martyr as opposed to a military hero, which has secular overtones.

In the fall of 2016, the presidential election campaigns of Donald Trump and Hillary Clinton were in full swing. The country was absolutely divided; the parties did not communicate with each other, and in some cases, campaign civility was completely put aside. The political environment was highly emotional and people took extreme positions—even among friends and family members. The media environment was somehow like that of the pre-television politically biased era of newspapers and readership leaned toward newspapers that were politically supportive. It only changed when three television networks ABC, CBS and NBC, decided to cater to members of both parties to expand their viewership to increase advertising revenue; American audiences were exposed to all versions of events from trustworthy and knowledgeable anchors such as Walter Cronkite, Edward Murrow, David Brinkley, and Peter Jennings.

Digital media technology, however, created countless outlets for people to receive information and opinion. Media became more and more segmented, catering to smaller and more politically and financially homogenous audiences in bubbles; CNN and MSNBC were more likely to support liberal views while Fox News and Newsmax were more on the side of conservative ideology. Traditional lines between news and opinion faded in many cases, and the distinction between true and false information was difficult for ordinary people to see. It seemed like we were back to selective exposure of the 1950s but with more emotional undertones and extremism due to personal and social characters of digital media. Many Iranians were rooting for Donald Trump since they liked his tough stance on Iran and were hopeful that he would change the Islamic regime there but were disappointed that President Trump had no such intention as he admired Putin who is firmly on the side of the Islamic regime.

This political division among people strongly manifested itself during the 2020 election campaigns that despite countless court rulings about the validity of President Biden's win and based on media disinformation, a large number of the electorate genuinely believed the election was stolen, thereby questioning the credibility and legitimacy of institutions that are the main pillars of democracy. Conspiracy theories abounded and led to a group of extremists to storm the Capitol building in the name of freedom and patriotic duties. I felt we came too close to be losing our freedom and democracy!

Watching television on Wednesday, January 6, 2021, brought back the memory of early February 1979 when the shah's armed forces collapsed and the people looted military bases. Ultimately, an extreme group of fanatical and uncompromising zealots took over the country. Of course, the January 6 insurrection was not comparable to the Iranian situation, mainly because the strength of American institutions is recognized by the majority of US citizens who agree that without it, there would be no democracy in America or the entire world.

Early in 2017, Iran was once again in the news. President Trump issued an executive order that placed stringent travel restrictions on citizens of Iran, prohibiting their entry to the United States to protect the US from foreign terrorists. Unfortunately, the ban instead of associating the government of Iran with terrorism branded anything Iranian as terrorist, once again bringing shame to innocent Iranian Americans, a harsh collective punishment that they didn't deserve. His decision to ban all Iranians from entering the US was made despite the lack of a notable history of terrorism on the part of Iranian people. For example, not one of the 9/11 terrorists who attacked the US was Iranian. I believe the ban was quite demoralizing for Iranian Americans, sending a message that they were not welcome in the United States.

During the summer of 2016, we flew to the crowded Heathrow Airport and then to Budapest, Hungary, where we spent about four nights in each city. I loved the Hungarian food and its rich history. We learned about the unbelievable destruction and brutality that was brought upon that country by Hitler and the old Soviet Union in a museum called the House of Horror. The museum was in a building that had been used by the Soviets and Nazis to interrogate, torture, and even execute people. Atrocities were documented on film and written material and the rooms were kept intact. Sadly, I hear there are many houses of horrors in Iran and in most authoritarian countries where human dignity and life is destroyed daily by the very same people getting paid by the public to protect them.

I learned that Hitler occupied Hungary in 1944 to prevent them from signing a separate armistice with the Western powers and the Soviets invaded Hungary in 1956 to crush their uprising and keep them under their domination by force. The Russian Empire, Soviet Union, and Russian Federation all have one thing in common—invading other countries! We saw quite a few castles and churches that had survived both occupations. I was quite surprised that after all those bitter experiences of fascism, the country was again moving toward extreme nationalism and isolationism in 2021.

We later went to Vienna, Austria's capital and stayed in the waterfront Hilton overlooking the blue Danube, but unfortunately, the river was brown. The intellectual and artistic legacy of the city was influenced by past residents including Sigmund

Freud, Beethoven, and Amadeus Mozart, whose "Marriage of Figaro" we enjoyed there while sipping champagne. It was fun! We also took a day trip and visited Salzburg where Mozart was born and "The Sound of Music" had been filmed. I had seen the movie, named "Tears and Smiles" in Farsi when in Iran. The song and movie were popular when I lived there.

Later we traveled to Prague, capital city of the Czech Republic. All my life, I had known the country as Czechoslovakia. It broke into two independent countries, the Czech Republic and the Slovak Republic. When I was in high school, Czechoslovakia had a trade show in Iran and left behind the warehouse type structure that housed their exhibition. The government used it for indoor sports like wrestling and ping pong matches.

Sherry and I stayed at the Waterfront Hilton on Vltava River along which we had many leisurely walks and on the famous Charles Bridge. In the evenings, we saw many young couples enjoying the romantic riverbank. Like most European cities, Prague has its share of magnificent castles and churches, but our most enjoyable activity in Prague was relaxing in the thermal water spa. After Prague, we flew to Berlin and saw the stark contrast in buildings that were mostly rebuilt under contrasting ideologies after the WWII in East and West Berlin. East Berlin buildings depicted grandiosity and uniformity like large buildings with small apartments, reflecting the collective nature of communism. Buildings on the west side utilized unique, individual designs using more green space, perhaps showing the individualistic culture of the West.

In January of 2017, Sherry and I took a Princess Cruise from Fort Lauderdale, Florida, to Cuba. A week before we left,

I got sick with the flu. An urgent care physician assistant prescribed some medication and told me that I would be okay. But on the ship, I started to cough terribly. On the first stop in Costa Maya, Mexico, Sherry and I went to buy a thermometer and perhaps some medication, but even after visiting four pharmacies by taxi, we could not find a thermometer—and the pharmacies had no medicine whatsoever! The place was so poor, I felt sorry for the people. I was surprised to see the people of a country that was supposed to be one of the main trading partners of the United States living in such dire conditions.

On the ship, a woman suggested that I take some cognac and lie in the sun. I tried it, but my cough got worse. At night, I remembered Alex Haley's book, *Roots: The Saga of an American Family* and how he described the awful the conditions under which slaves were transported by ship from Africa to America. One condition for traveling to Cuba as an American was for educational purposes. To qualify, we had to purchase an excursion ticket for learning Cuban dances; they took us to a depilated house to dance with a group of Cuban senior citizens for about 30 minutes to satisfy the educational condition for entering Cuba.

In Havana, we visited the house where Ernest Hemingway lived in the 1940s. I had read *The Old Man and the Sea* when I was learning English and loved the simplicity of his writing. It was exciting to see where a man who won the Pulitzer Prize twice worked and lived. Other than lots of refurbished cars from the 1950s and several bars for tourists, I didn't see much in Havana.

A highlight of the trip was visiting Santa Clara, the capital city of the Cuban province of Villa Clara. The city is associated with Ernesto "Che" Guevara, a leader of the revolution and a war hero. He was an icon and role model for many young Marxist militant communist rebels in Iran and around the world who were motivated and inspired by a false communist vison. Santa Clara was where the revolutionaries under the command of Che Guevara defeated General Fulgencio Batista's soldiers, including the ones in an armored train, resulting in the fall of Santa Clara and Batista's subsequent escape from Cuba in 1959. I couldn't help comparing Che with Ghasem Soleimani, a commander of a branch of the Islamic Republic revolutionary guard corps in charge of unconventional warfare and extraterritorial operations in Iran, Quds Force. Both men were revolutionary leaders and war heroes passionate about exporting their respective revolutions to foreign countries and were often involved in foreign internal wars supporting Russia and opposing the US and its allies. They both were charismatic and often upstaged their own leaders by receiving more applause and cheers from the crowds. Finally, they both were assassinated outside of their countries with the help of CIA and the United States military. Che Guevara was killed in Bolivia in 1967, and Soleimani was killed in Iraq more than three decades later in 2020. Today, both Cuba and Iran are isolated and have warm relations with Russia, the United States' foremost adversary.

The tour bus took us through the countryside where the dilapidated homes and poor surroundings were depressing. It was so sad that the people of Cuba remained impoverished no matter who ruled them. Cuba was a Spanish colony for four centuries, came under American military control after 1898, and eventually, was under Castro's communist regime.

In May 2018, Professor Chun Yang Hu invited me to go to Shanghai to teach in a summer seminar at Fudan University. Dr. Hu, whose American name is Spring, had spent some time at Fullerton as an international scholar and Sherry and I had developed a friendship with her. It was my second trip to Shanghai but this time, Sherry was with me and we both were amazed by how the city had transformed in general; the progress was magical! I took Sherry to the Bund one night and we had a pleasant walk along the bank of the Huangpu River. The panoramic view of the illuminated traditional buildings on one side and modern skyscrapers lights on the other side of the river was symbolically honoring both the past and present.

I did not see the army of bicycles that I had on my previous trip, but I did see lots of motor scooters with two adults and a child, all riding without helmets. When Sherry asked one of the Chinese doctoral students why the authorities didn't make it illegal to ride without a helmet, the student responded, "Strong laws don't work!" I thought her answer was pretty smart given that millions of people depended on scooters for their daily transportation, not to mention the production and cost of that many helmets. I guess it would be hard to enforce that type of law for millions of people in a hot and humid environment.

Contrary to my expectation of an authoritarian professor-student relationship in China, Professor Chun Yang Hu and her students were genuinely cordial, the students spoke English well and were quite knowledgeable about world affairs. On our way to having lunch in the student cafeteria, I noticed an office next to the dean's that was the same size. I was told it was the ideological authority's office to keep all academic activities in line. I heard Iran was using the same system and that a cleric was placed in all government and military offices for guidance! I also saw Halal meat served, despite what I had heard about the Chinese's disrespecting Muslims.

We traveled to Hangzhou and Nanjing, two very beautiful ancient cities, especially Nanjing, which had been China's capital city during the Ming dynasty. We had lengthy conversations with the two doctoral students accompanying us about China's old and rich culture, their own educational experience, and their intellectual development. It seemed in China, education was much more holistic than the United States, although they follow the US model in some areas.

During my last class before I fully retired in the spring of 2019, I was pleasantly surprised when my students brought a cake with my name on it and took pictures with me. It was a sweet gesture that I will always remember. There were other parties too; my former chair and friend Tony Fellow held a nice reception for me in his beautiful home which quite a few of my colleagues attended. Also, Mike and Melody organized a large reception at Mike and Alice's home in Redondo Beach and invited the entire family living in Southern California, including my two brothers, Melody and Brian, my sister, nephews, nieces, and friends. Alice had made a poster saying, "A legend Is Retiring," and Melody gave a little talk. I was so humbled and appreciated their thoughtfulness.

In December of 2019, we started hearing about patients in Wuhan, China, who were experiencing shortness of breath and fever. The illness quickly spread around the world, and in late January 2020, the World Health Organization (WHO) declared COVID-19 a public health emergency caused by

SARS. Most of us were following recommendations of the CDC in wearing face masks, maintaining at least a six-foot distance, and regularly washing our hands. In March 2020, California's Governor Newsom ordered Californians to stay home; parks and public places were closed. Everybody was avoiding other people because of the fear of getting infected. Sherry and I went to Laguna Beach one evening and could not believe how a vibrant city was deserted and no public restrooms were open—something that we had not thought about before leaving home! It was quite painful not being able to visit our children and grandchildren whom we love so much to hug and kiss them. We were just too afraid to catch the disease and the only way that we could see our friends and family was through video calls. Boring online poker replaced our lively game with my friends. We used PokerStars' Home Games and communicated through Google Meet and settled our accounts with Zelle. The game was too fast and was void of personal interactions with friends in a social setting. It was only after COVID-19 vaccinations that we got together again and played, initially with masks on.

Our close neighbors, Roberta and Kathy, Carl and Lori, and Jim and Helen decided to meet every Saturday at 5 p.m. We would put chairs and a small table with wine on our driveway. Lori, our next-door neighbor, is quite resourceful in entertainment. Every week, she had new bingo boards and other games like throwing darts where every couple was a team and the winners received special trophies that Lori's husband Carl made in his garage. Sherry and I won several trophies. When it got dark, Lori brought out her Alexa speaker and we all drank and danced on the street, observing the six-foot distance recommendation.

During a summer teaching at Fudan University. On my right is Professor Chun Yang Hu and on my left is Sherry, Shanghai, China in 2018.

With my extended family at the premier of " A Simple wedding," directed by my niece Sara Zandieh, the fifth from the left on the back row. Los Angeles, California, September 2018.

My grandkids love Starbucks. From the left is Sophia, Ben, Brandon. Elliott and me.

Visiting Lyon Air Museum with my grandkids Elliot and Brandon in Orange County, California 2018.

Our granddaughter Sophia with b.b. when she is twelve around 2022.

During 2023 Christmas holidays in San Diego, California. From Left: Sherry, our grandson Ben, Melody, grandson Brandon, son-in-law, Brian, grandson Elliott and me.

My cousin Negar from Germany and her children are visiting with Sherry's brother, Simon Tavassoli, President of B.B. Simon at his company in Irvine California during summer of 2023. From left is Nami, Simon, Nava, and Negar.

Alice, my daughter-in-law with Sophia at her graduation from Adams Middle School, where She received an outstanding academic achievement award. Redondo Beach, California, 2024.

During the 2020 presidential elections, the pandemic became a hot political issue. President Trump was trying to protect the economy by playing down the pandemic while health scientists were trying to save lives by playing up the seriousness of the disease, educating the public about the dangers of it. This was a confusing and risky time; we occasionally heard about people we knew who were severely ill or passed away because of COVID-19. We stopped going to the gym, avoided eating out, and did not travel.

In the meantime, in Orange County, many people were infected and hospitals were out of ICU beds, ventilators, and equipment to care for pandemic patients. My neighbor across the street got sick during his honeymoon in Hawaii and the couple was quarantined in an expensive hotel room until they could return. I encouraged my neighbor to go to the hospital, but the University of Irvine hospital was not able to help him since it was out of space; a makeshift tent was set up on the sidewalk, and after sitting there for hours, he went home without anyone helping him. Similar stories of sickness and death abounded.

In August of 2020, my 96-year-old mom died peacefully a few months after she had a fall. It was so sad that only a few of us could attend her funeral due to COVID-19 restrictions. She always made me feel special with her warm smile and encouraging words. As we were growing up, she tirelessly followed up our academic progress by talking to our teachers and helping us with our homework. Despite her own challenges and setbacks, she always gave us her full attention, kept us entertained, and made us feel loved and appreciated. When I was in ninth grade, I was a member of the Red Lion and Sun Society that was affiliated with Red Cross and Red Crescent societies. On very short notice, our teacher announced that we all had to participate in a parade the next morning in formal regalia that included a dark blue beret, dark blue pants, a white shirt, and a dark blue tie. I had none of the items but very much wanted to participate in the parade so after dinner that evening, I mentioned it to my mom. By then, most shops were closed, but my mom took me around Tehran by bus, taxi, and on foot, even visiting the home of a store owner until she could buy all the items I needed. I was so excited and thankful. My sister Fariba, as her only daughter, was truly the apple of Mom's eye! Sadly, several months after my mom's passing, we suddenly lost our sister Fariba to cancer. She had been a breast cancer survivor, but around 2017, she was diagnosed with stage four lung cancer for which she was taking medication. Her early death was quite painful, especially since she looked quite normal until a few weeks before she passed. I was around 10 when our mom had Fariba and was the first person in our entire family to have regular birthday celebrations with cakes, candles, and pictures. Our mother helped Fariba to become a US citizen and spent most of her life close to her as Fariba divorced in her early 30s but worked hard to raise her two kids alone.

Sherry and I got vaccinated by February so we could resume both our biannual reunion in Vegas and in-person poker games. Pandemic restrictions were everywhere, and in Vegas, casinos strictly enforced mask-wearing and had installed plexiglass shields between players to minimize transmission. During the summer of 2021, my niece Sara Zandieh had her engagement party in Maryland at the Kentland Mansion near the city of Gaithersburg, about 40 minutes from Washington National

Cathedral. The venue was also used as an art gallery, the perfect place to see our East Coast family members after a long time. We are all proud of Sara, who is an award-winning TV and film director. One of her early works was a documentary about Iranian underground musical groups for MTV. She also did a feature film called " A Simple Wedding" among others, including the NBC one-hour series *Good Girls*.

Quite a few people were at the party, so when we got back to my cousin Shane's house, we panicked and thought about how we should not have traveled from California to Maryland. We took a whole bunch of vitamin C and gargled mouthwash. We learned that a few people, including a couple who were wearing masks and refused to even shake hands with anyone, had tested positive for COVID-19 and became severely ill after the party. There was a little family feud and finger-pointing about who brought the virus to the party. By October 2021, the CDC approved the vaccines for children five years and older, but no one I knew had their kids vaccinated. Quite a few Iranian Americans had joined the anti-vaccine groups and none of them vaccinated their kids. There were countless stories of our friends and family in Iran who got COVID-19 with severe symptoms.

Right after the pandemic came under control somewhat in 2022, we witnessed a major clash between the Islamic Republic's regime and the young people in Iran; the demonstrations were especially fueled by female high school and college students who mostly appeared without the Islamic hijab. The elderly ruling clerics considered hijab a symbol of political and religious solidarity with the regime and required women to wear a long shawl, a *chador*, to completely cover their hair and the curvature of their body. Since the Pahlavi dynasty was overthrown, the regime constantly worked to make the hijab an integral part of Iranian culture through multifaceted campaigns in schools, mosques, morality classes, and the media. They also spent the equivalent of millions of dollars to establish a morality police with monitoring equipment and cameras around the country to enforce the hijab rule.

Based on my conversations with Iranians, it seems investigations and prosecutions related to major crimes such as robbery, fraud, and drug and human trafficking are taking a back seat to the enforcement of the hijab. But in the age of the social media and the internet, it is almost impossible to force most young Iranian urban women to wear a hijab in all public places.

In September 2022, Mahsa Amini, a young Iranian woman, died in the custody of the so-called morality police in Tehran; soon millions of young women led weeks of nationwide protests in solidarity with Mahsa who had been arrested for merely wearing her headscarf too loosely. Her death also sparked worldwide demonstrations for freedom in Iran against the Islamic Republic and its leaders. The demonstrations provided opportunities for young people to express major grievances such as inflation, the mismanagement and corruption in the government, air and water pollution, and lack of employment opportunities.

Shervin Hajipoor, an Iranian singer and songwriter summed it up in the song "Baraye" meaning because, reflecting the despair and agony of the young people in Iran who were yearning for freedom and a simple, ordinary life with dignity and peace. The song went viral and many versions were performed in languages around the world, including at President Biden's White House, by invitation of his wife, Dr. Jill Biden. It became the national anthem of women in Iran with the slogan of "Woman, Life, Freedom."

Soon after Shervin wrote the song, he was arrested and jailed. The two journalists who broke the story of Mahsa, Niloofar Hamedi and Elaheh Mohammadi, have been in the notorious Evin Prison and have talked about their mistreatment and abuse in custody. The Islamic Republic accused the West of fomenting protests and proceeded to violently crack down the demonstrations by using live ammunition, metal pellets, and rubber bullets. In American and international media, we saw many grieving parents at the funerals of their children who were among as many as five hundred (estimated by the media) young men and women killed during demonstrations. Many others had been left with ruptured eyes and metal pellets in their bodies. A score of others were arrested, and after sham trials, were later executed. Huge crowds chanted anti-regime slogans in solidarity with the families, either at the funerals or in front of Evin Prison despite the regime's efforts to keep them quiet. In addition, during the eight-month uprising, security forces arrested countless young people, especially women, subjecting them to horrific torture and sexual abuse that was recounted by those who were freed. Major US and international media reported that after protests died down, many female students were mysteriously poisoned in their high schools around the country, a heinous crime still unresolved in 2024, when Shervin Hajipoor was arrested again and, according to some media reports, was asked to write anti-American songs.

In 2022, as the Islamic Republic was killing and maiming lawful protesters demanding their basic human rights, it sent hundreds of drones capable of suicide bombings to partner with Russia in killing tens of thousands of innocent Ukrainian civilians. In 2023, resistance to wearing a hijab became a symbol protesting religious dictatorship, especially for urban women around the country, and the enforcement of hijabs again became the focus of the government of the Islamic Republic. Despite the constant tension and disruptions in the country, young Iranians have made incredible strides in science, technology, and medicine, as well as the arts while the ruling clerics has failed miserably in their basic task of establishing morality and social justice in the country.

It was heartening to see the international community support those protesting the totalitarian regime in Iran. Iranian journalists Niloofar Hamedi and Elaheh Mohammadi who helped publicize news about Mahsa Amini's death were awarded WAN-IFRSA's 2023 Golden Pen of Freedom, and *Time* magazine named both journalists among the 100 most influential people of 2023. Hajipoor received the Best Song for Social Change Award at the 2023 Grammy's for his song. The 2023 Nobel Peace Prize was awarded to journalist and activist Narges Mohammadi for her persistent fight against the oppression of women by the Islamic Republic of Iran.

On October 7, 2023, Hamas forces launched an unprecedented attack inside Israel, killing more than one thousand people and taking about 240 hostages. It was unnoticed by most countries that the Islamic Republic had been training and arming Hamas fighters along with its other proxy forces in Iraq, Syria, Yemen, and Lebanon, spending billions of dollars over the years. Immediately after the attack, Ayatollah Khamenei congratulated the attackers and mentioned that he would kiss their "arms" and "foreheads." Other Iranian officials indirectly took credit for the attack and an IRGC spokesperson characterized the attack as revenge for the assassination of Ghasem Soleimani, but it was denied by Hamas. Later, commander-in-chief of the IRGC Hossein Salami refuted previous comments and vehemently denied that Iran was directly involved. In response to the attack and in pursuit of destroying Hamas forces, the ultra-right government of Israel launched a ferocious attack inside Gaza, by land, sea and air, flattening most buildings and killing thirty thousand people, including many innocent women and children. The Gazans expected their benefactor, Iran, to come to their rescue in their hour of need and probably were wondering whether the Islamic Republic of Iran really meant their chants of "Death to Israel!" during past four plus decades. Of course, the Islamic Republic was unable to face a direct, armed conflict with Israel and the United States, primarily due to the significant US firepower in the region and a demoralized and dissatisfied Iranian public as was evidenced by massive demonstrations in 2022.

To maintain its credibility and legitimacy, the Islamic Republic instructed its proxies in Iraq and Syria to keep attacks on US interests in the region symbolic and low-leveled, and asked Lebanon's Hezbollah to limit its attacks on the border between Lebanon and Israel. When Israel's defense forces laid siege to the Gaza Strip depriving the entire Gaza population of food, water, and fuel, Ayatollah Khamenei said on television that they must stop food and fuel from reaching Israel. But things did not go according to plan when three US soldiers were killed and about 40 were injured around the Jordan–Syria border by a coalition of Iran-linked groups in Iraq. The

Iran-backed Houthis initially tried to hit Israeli-bound ships from Yaman but ended up randomly hitting ships in the Red Sea, threatening the international commerce. They have also attacked US warships and recently sank a ship carrying fertilizer that could cause an environmental disaster. In the meantime, the Islamic Republic of Iran is fully pursuing nuclear technology and production and is still exporting drones and missiles to Russia in support of its war with Ukraine.

On April 13, 2024, Iran launched more than three hundred drones and missiles, apparently in retaliation for Israel's strike on an Iranian embassy two weeks prior, but most were intercepted by Israel, the US, and Jordan.

The New York Times reported that experts believed it was the first time Iran attacked Israel from Iranian territory—and with weapons that were more sophisticated than others recently fired at Israel. In support of Israel, President Biden planned a meeting with the G7 (Group of Seven) leaders, an intergovernmental political and economic forum. The event brought Iran's shadow war against Israel into the open. The question now is whether the conflict will return to its previous long-running shadow war or enter a more dangerous new stage.

In May 2024, *Reuters* reported that Iranian President Ebrahim Raisi was killed in a helicopter crash. His death during rising Middle East tensions will most certainly result in much uncertainty about the future of Iran and the region. Unfortunately, his misguided and reckless policies and those of the ultra-frail and corrupt leaders of the Islamic Republic have brought Iran, a country rich in human and natural resources, to the precipice of poverty, civil strife, and war.

As I end this story, Sherry and I celebrate our golden anniversary. I surprised her with a trip to Amsterdam where we visited Keukenhof, the most beautiful tulip garden in the world, during the tulip festival. We feel the tulip is a befitting symbol as it signifies perfect and deep love.

Although I love the land of my birth, its culture, and its customs, I am happy to be an American citizen and enjoy the freedom and the relative safety of the United States.

Sherry and I are celebrating our gold anniversary in Keukenhof, Netherland during their Tulip Festival, April 2024.

AUTHOR'S NOTES

Fred Zandpour was born in Tehran, Iran. During 1970s, he was the managing director of Admen-BBDO in Tehran with a client list that included Exxon, Bristol Myers, and Colgate Palmolive. After the Islamic Revolution, he immigrated to the United States with his family and earned a master's degree from the University of Portland and a doctoral degree from the University of Washington Seattle. He launched his academic career, initially at Penn State and then at Cal State, becoming a professor and dean. He focused his energy on promoting international communication and integrating digital technology into his educational efforts. Fred earned numerous congressional commendations, as well as state and local certificates of recognition. President George Bush and Senator Dianne Feinstein congratulated Fred for winning the US Small Business Award in 2008 that recognized his educational contributions. He facilitated successful international educational programs in Europe and Asia, and his research on international advertising—widely published in US and UK journals—was one of the top ten most cited sources in the US for 10 years.

His wife, Sherry, received a master's degree from Penn State University and their children, Mike and Melody, are successful corporate lawyers. Now retired, Fred enjoys time with his grandchildren, Sophia, Elliott, Brandon, and Ben. He is grateful for the experience of having taught, advised, and mentored thousands of American college students over his three decades in education.

ACKNOWLEDGMENTS

I would like to thank Heather Pendley for her superb editing and guidance. Special thanks also to Teija Lammi who meticulously designed the interior of the book and for adjustment and formatting of the cover. I am also grateful for WJ Byrun's work on the cover design.

I wish to express my deepest appreciation to my wife, Sherry, who supported me with great patience and understanding while I was working on this project and who has put up with me for the past 50 years.